The Art of Assessment

Laura Middleton

VENTURE PRESS

Published by
VENTURE PRESS
16 Kent Street
Birmingham
B5 6RD

British Library Cataloguing-in-Publication Data
A catalogue record for this book is available from the British Library

ISBN 1 873878 87 7   (paperback)

Design, layout and production by
Hucksters Advertising & Publishing Consultants,
Riseden, Tidebrook, Wadhurst, East Sussex TN5 6PA

Cover design by:
Western Arts
194 Goswell Road
London
EC1V 7DT

Printed in Great Britain

Contents

Acknowledgements

As ever, I am indebted to my friends:

Ann Gegg and Ruth Eley for being the best back up team anyone could ever want or need.

Kamlesh Patel, for all the time spent sharing his ideas and enthusiasm with me.

Sally Arkley ... without whose persistent encouragement...!

Assessment is too big a topic for such a short book. I am grateful to the other authors in this series for covering so many of the areas to which I am unable to do justice.

LAURA MIDDLETON
1997

Introduction: a question of balance

Assessment is not viewed as a benign process by many of those it is aimed at and in social welfare terms it is a process which seems to happen to the socially disadvantaged. Social workers, among others, have become conceptualised by some as the new agents of social control, as government has concerned itself more with the behaviour, health and welfare of

> " I'm governed by a gang of fanatical dogmatists, all determined that everyone shall be continually assessed from the moment of his or her first day at school until the inevitable oblivion of a private nursing home.
> I don't like it"
> **Letter to The Independent from a 75-year-old, quoted by Denise Platt [1990]**

the population. Black people may be particularly suspicious of the motives of local authority assessors, and interpret the process as yet another means of pathologising their experience by white-run agencies.

This negative feeling may be shared by disabled people of non-disabled assessors; old people of young ones, or children of adults. I could go on. Assessment, at its worst, is the exercise of power by one section of society over another. Organisations need to be aware and sensitive to these issues, and address them.

Assessment is not about judging a person, but about getting to know them and their situation, with the intent of changing it for the better. This book undertakes to develop an understanding of the purpose and process of assessment, to interpret it as a professional activity that forms part of helping, and to describe the pressures and constraints that operate against it being a helpful activity.

Undeniably, assessment can serve an organisational agenda which is not in the best interests of the consumer. Furthermore, it is an unpalatable fact that much assessment, judged in professional terms, is very badly done and its purpose ill understood. The way forward lies in rediscovering and promoting the purpose of welfare organisations – to improve people's situations – and convincing those currently in the driving seat that this is entirely compatible with being effective and efficient. Nor, despite the hysteria of the new right, will an effective welfare service undermine the fabric of society.

Building faith in the effectiveness of welfare services means finding ways of restoring confidence both in professional judgement and in that of individuals about their own situations. This will not be easy while so many 'professionals' behave like institutionalised automatons, resulting in a lack of trust from the people in whose interests they should be acting. It follows that those charged with assessment need an intelligent understanding of its purpose; its context; and its potential to harm as well as to help, in addition to having the skills that enable assessment to be carried out. They also need the confidence to be assertive within their organisations and to achieve the credibility to engage in pressing for changes in practice.

It is essential for organisations to examine their practices around racism and other means of oppression. The existence of equal opportunity policies and statements, however prettily packaged, is insufficient. What matters is the implementation in service terms and a willingness to recognise and deal with oppressive practices. Organisations have to develop positive strategies which are realistic not token, establish appropriate services and dispel assumptions that health and welfare services are only for white people, or heterosexuals, or those who live on the moral high ground in traditional nuclear families.

This is admittedly all very difficult in the face of so much societal and organisational pressure to discriminate.

Nevertheless, professional workers owe it to their clients to think their way through these complexities and try to make the social welfare system work as well as they can. This includes working with health and other agencies and being aware of their differing cultures and priorities. Consciousness of resource constraints means making the system work for all potential users, and not just for those individual clients for whom workers see themselves 'acting' on a legal model. The adoption of the term 'service user' moves the concept towards a wider acceptance of responsibility for equity in service distribution, and improvements that affect everyone.

This means that the best deal for the many may mean sacrificing the ideal deal for the few. As such, assessment becomes as much a managerial balancing act as a professional advocacy role. As it leaves such concepts behind and adopts a wider role in the management of welfare, individualistic social work is evolving into care management.

A successful care manager is someone who is able to see all sides of the picture, and can take a strategic view, to achieve the best deal for all potential service users, most of whom are less eloquent than the angry man thumping the reception desk, and less time consuming than the woman instituting judicial review. It would be a pity if fear of either of these individuals meant they dictated the terms for the majority of service users.

Despite the uncomfortable charges of being agents of social control, there is surely still a case to be made for a state-led redistribution of resources from well-off to less well off, other than through the mechanisms of crime. Achieving some sort of balance which ensures state help to vulnerable people without over-regulation or interference is no easy matter, and involves taking a stance which is much more complex than either of the opposing ideological standpoints which favour either state control or the free market.

This leads us to a new concept of what is meant by assessment. It is not simply an activity conducted between professional and client to come up with some kind of personal development plan, or a wish list of service provision. If assessment is to be a purposeful activity, it has to be more than that. Assessment is the art of managing competing demands, and negotiating the most reasonable outcome. It means steering between the clashing rocks of organisational demand; legislative dictates; limited resources; political and personal agendas. It includes having the confidence to keep on one's feet in an inter-agency setting when the ground beneath them is constantly shifting. It is about making sense of the situation as a whole, and working out the best way to achieve change.

Good social workers undergoing this metamorphosis will nevertheless wish to retain their commitments to anti-discriminatory practice as a value base, the right of all adults and children to inclusion within society and the ideal of social justice. Such practitioners will wish to work through the assessment and care management system to challenge oppression actively at both personal and institutional levels. This will not happen by accident. It means making a conscious effort to include people at all stages in their own assessment. High quality assessment cannot be achieved without a value base which respects individual rights, and yet we have to work within a system which does not.

This may entail us in a very tricky juggling act, but unless social workers do develop such skills assessment will deteriorate into a dehumanising system of routinely shifting people like so many parcels along the conveyer belt of the care continuum. It is a question of balance.

What is assessment?

I have encountered too many people who make remarks like: 'I've been to assess Mrs Green' or 'Mr Brown did very well at his assessment' to feel easy about not stating what to many will be obvious. It is not, of course, Mrs Green or Mr Brown who are the rightful subjects of the assessment, but the situations in which they find themselves. The difference is crucial, and will influence the way in which the assessment is approached and consequently experienced by the service user.

Assessment is the analytical process by which decisions are made. In a social welfare context, it is a basis for planning what needs to be done to maintain or improve a person's situation, although it is not the plan itself. Still less is it the organisational arrangements which will be made to put the plan into operation, but the assessor will need to know that such arrangements are possible and acceptable before surrendering responsibility for the assessment. Assessment involves gathering and interpreting information in order to understand a person and their circumstances; the desirability and feasibility of change and the services and resources which are necessary to effect it. It involves making judgements based on information.

Social workers, or others undertaking assessment, should understand it as an exercise with purpose, and not simply a directionless conversation or interaction. This does not mean substituting set routines, or indulging in standardised questioning at the expense of open listening. Nor, crucially, does it mean the collection of vast amounts of data as if its collection had some intrinsic merit. There is nothing meritritous in persuading people to share information they would prefer to keep confidential unless its revelation serves some purpose. Gathering data which is not pertinent to the situation is intrusive and an invasion of privacy, as well as a waste of time.

Veronica Coulshed noted that beginners tended to use what she called a 'scatter gun method', hoping to find out something worthwhile by asking more and more questions, but resulting in confusion from information overload (Coulshed 1988). She believed that the skill of assessment lay in the ability to collect the right kind of information, and to remember that we can never know all there is to know about people or systems. Assessments are dynamic processes that can never be complete, true or comprehensive. The skill is in knowing when enough information has been collected and considered to move toward making plans with the person whose situation is being assessed. Assessment is not an exact science and the ability to make judgements about people's circumstances is a mixture of experience and the ability to reflect on it.

Potential service users should be encouraged to share this understanding about assessment as a dynamic, imperfect process, and to understand that we will never know all there is to know. Most people understand that there is a limited resource pot, and that there are waiting lists and costs to consider. Nor do they wish control over their lives to be removed from them: it is not possible, nor desirable, to legislate away all risk. What they may need to have explained is the priorities of particular organisations, and where they stand in relation to such priorities. This enables choices to be made on realistic information. Casualty departments often have a waiting time displayed, against which a person with a minor injury can make their own judgement about the worth of the wait. Housing departments often have different length lists for different standards of property or area.

It is still rare for social services to be so upfront about service availability, nor are service users yet adequately respected as consumers. The new Community Care charters are typically more likely to concentrate on such things as response times and processes of assessment than on the levels of help people can expect to receive, although wary local authorities are insuring against complaints by building in early caveats about the costs they will bear.

Information gathered, and the use made of it, should be openly available to the person whose situation is being assessed, even if the information is sometimes unpalatable. Assessment should be an inclusive process, centring on an individual or group, but focusing on their situation. It is a participative activity, with the intent of identifying feasible and reasonable plans for change which improve the quality of people's lives. Being realistic does not deny people the opportunity to dream: indeed, sharing dreams is as good a way as any of opening the proceedings.

If Mrs Green and Mr Brown feel threatened by the prospect of assessment, the messages about what it means are wrong. Social workers need to bear constantly in mind that asking for help is difficult. It may be the tenth time that day they have been in an assessment process, but it may well be Mrs Green's first time! On the other hand, the social worker may be the fourth person who has come to assess Mrs Green in as many days! We cannot avoid the fact that people encounter social workers when there are difficulties, but we can make it less stigmatic by emphasising its normality, and the rights of people to expect support.

A further imperfection built into an overstretched welfare system is the expected shelf life of assessments, many of which rapidly pass their sell-by date. In practice, assessment has to be completed in the short term and can only remain 'true' in the short term. Nevertheless, it probably has to relate to provision in the long term, given most departments' inability to review. This means making predictive judgements about what is likely to occur in the future. Such predictions are based on experiences of what has happened in similar circumstances. The individual nature of assessments is in danger of getting lost in such a climate, and the worker has to seek to achieve a balance.

Since the National Health Service and Community Care Act of 1990 (NHS&CC Act) it is crystal clear that assessment is no longer an option but, under Section 47, a legal duty.

We could spend some time arguing that, had local authorities chosen to interpret previous legislation differently, assessment would have been regarded as a duty for some time and responded to as such. The administrative exclusion of people over 60 from the category of 'disabled', for example, has meant that they have rarely been offered assessment under Section 4 of the

1986 Disabled Persons Act, despite the obvious fact that social services come into contact with older people because of their ill health or disability and not because of their age.

Indeed, invoking the 1986 Act is still the best legal way of ensuring a comprehensive assessment by a local authority for anyone over 18 who appears to be disabled, irrespective of the scale of need initially presented. Conceptualising themselves as disabled may be a hurdle for some people, but it could avoid their being sidelined into a 'simple assessment' by an untrained worker. But perhaps that is another story... suffice it to say that assessment is not a **new** legal requirement on local authorities, nor is it new practice. Social workers have always assessed children, foster carers, people with mental health problems and so on, but since it hit the mainstream in the form of the NHS&CC Act, assessment has acquired its high profile, its capital A, and its association with major-league restructuring.

It has also become narrowly prescribed as an activity. Assessment used to mean simply appraising a situation and was an interwoven part of any social worker's relationship with their client. It was not an activity confined to some workers defined as 'assessors' or belonging to assessment teams, and it did not rely on standardised data or formula. Its quality was openly acknowledged as dependent on the skill and thoroughness of the assessor: unlike the current situation, where there is a growing and, in my view, dangerous belief that the quality of assessment owes more to the quality of the assessment tools in use, or worse still, to the quantity of data collected.

The process laid down in the Act clearly makes a difference between the assessment and the provision of service which may follow from it, which means the assessment can exist irrespective of the ability or the intention of the relevant authority to provide service. Many local authorities have enthusiastically reorganised themselves to operate along these lines. It is a legally tenable position: indeed, it offers a wealth of opportunity for lawyers to exploit the gap created. It is clearly desirable for the assessor to maintain a conceptual distinction between need and service availability, but professionally, it is nonsense to undertake assessment as an activity divorced from seeking a reasonable response to meeting the individual's requirements. It is arguably also professionally unethical to do so.

In health care terms a doctor should consider not only the simple relationship between a disease and a cure, but the patient's ability to comply with treatment, its availability and affordability, before recommending it as the most appropriate course to take. Social work judgements are no less complicated: indeed the evidence may be even less tangible. It is essential that professional helpers remain alive to their responsibilities to the individual concerned, seek realistic and acceptable ways forward and deal honestly and openly with everyone concerned.

The Social Services Inspectorate is very clear in its recommendation to separate assessment from care planning, and notes in its reports the numbers of authorities who remain confused about this (SSI 1995). Assessment is the process by which decisions are made about the sort of services people need and can expect: care planning is the detailed information about what exactly the services should consist of. This model is derived from hospital discharge where the assessment is envisaged as dictating the desirability or otherwise of a residential or nursing home, and ends with a recommendation of which home. Care planning is then a distinct process which follows on from the assessment, and could be carried out by different personnel. In practice this second stage of the process often does not happen at all.

The Care Plan, in my view, should be the outcome of the assessment, despite the practical difficulties this currently poses for many assessment teams both in terms of the time they have available, and their often limited ability to draw up feasible plans.

Common sense dictates that some of the organisational details of exactly how and what will be provided remain the day-to-day responsibility of the service providers. But unless the assessment ends with an agreed plan, it will be impossible either to review the decision, or ensure that any quality control mechanisms are in place. The choice of a residential home is insufficient, therefore. The assessment should provide recommendations about the level and type of care needed, and any specific needs the individual may have, as well as making arrangements about how the plan will be reviewed. These have to be drawn up and agreed with all the service providers. Whether it is a contract, service agreement or care plan, the document which is the final product of the assessment is the handover from assessment to service provision. It is best envisaged as the sort of handover which occurs in a relay race, where the athletes run alongside each other for a while, hopefully passing the baton in the process!

It is an underlying contention of this book that professionals and organisations must find a way to extend the responsibility in undertaking assessment to include the negotiation of feasible resource provision. If they do not, service users will become discontented and disillusioned, local authorities will face an increasing volume of litigation, and the whole process will sink into disrepute. This means professionals, the organisations for whom they work and their political masters reaching a more reasonable accommodation about what can be done than is often the case at present. This could be reached in consultation with service users, who know that there are restrictions on resources, and who can help in agreeing how they might best be allocated.

THE OFFICIAL VERSION

Understanding the official view of what assessment should be forms a basis for developing ways of working which are within the legislation, and for informed criticism.

For the beginner wishing to fathom the task as envisaged by the policy makers, *The Practitioners Guide to Care Management and Assessment* is designed as an accessible source (HMSO 1991). It emphasises four major themes:

● Services should be fitted to need, not vice versa. The service outcome, in other words, should not be pre-supposed in the initial responses

● Assessing need should be separated from the delivery of service

- A revision of organisational structures and change of managerial attitude and approach are needed

- The empowerment of users and carers is a key concept.

The Social Services Inspectorate adds its own standards for assessment in the 1991 Guide 'Getting the Message Across'

Assessment should:

- recognise that some users may be the best assessors of their own needs and solutions

- consider the needs and strengths of individuals in the context of their everyday lives

- be separate from a decision about allocation of services

- strike a balance between invading privacy and obtaining sufficient information

- recognise the rights of carers to a separate assessment

- be ethnically and culturally sensitive.
(SSI 1991)

Most of these expectations are reinforced in the Guidance to the Children Act which stresses that people should not be assessed to fit existing services, but that services should be adapted to meet need. Social services are instructed to provide information about services, and about the assessment procedures that have been put in place to determine need.

The quarrel with these expectations rests less on the notion of a needs-led service, but on the understanding of need that underpins it. We might usefully compare the government definition with an understanding informed by anti-oppressive practice.

Rightly, the Government tells us that need is a complex concept which has been analysed in a variety of ways, but as far as they are concerned it means :

> 'a shorthand for the requirements of
> individuals to enable them to achieve,
> maintain or restore an acceptable level of
> social independence or quality of life, as
> defined by the particular care agency or
> authority'
> **(Practitioners Guide p12, HMSO 1991)**

The sting is in the tail: need is relative, and locally defined.

An anti-oppressive stance would hold that a person's need relates not simply to requirements to 'achieve, maintain or restore' but is, crucially, about the removal of artificial obstacles and barriers which prevent or hinder adults or children from achieving normal goals related to their age and ability. In fact, it might be more helpful to delete the concept of need altogether, given its tendency to be professionally determined, and substitute rights or aspirations. Key concepts are: partnership with parents and children; listening to children; and not making assumptions based on categories of disability.

The dynamics of need and demand are more fully discussed later.

The National Health Service and Community Care Act 1990 moves assessment very clearly from what it calls 'service-led' to 'needs-led'. This is within the overall intention of government policy to separate the assessment for services from service provision itself, in an attempt to extend the sources of provision and develop a mixed economy of welfare. For which, if you like, you could read reducing the share of the public sector and promoting growth in the private and voluntary fields. Freeing assessment from its direct link with service provision was intended to widen the possibilities for using services within a marketplace culture. There are a great many flaws in the argument, not least of which is the incompatibility of a needs-led purchasing model with restricted resources. Difficulties in splitting these functions has arisen in both health and social services because many of the necessary skills concerning assessment and the matching of need to resources lie with providers. Accordingly, most purchasers do not have an intimate enough knowledge about the detail of services, what they can and cannot do, and how flexible they can be. Nor is this situation improving: as time goes on the evidence is that purchasers get even less clear about service provision **(Common and Flynn 1992)**. Competing providers in the new culture sometimes seem to devote more organisational energy to marketing and packaging themselves than they do to ensuring genuine quality of product. It is therefore crucial that assessors at least remain very clear about their end of the business: what the individual concerned requires. Without such commitment from assessors, those on the receiving end will quickly become hapless victims of hard-sell, despite the rhetoric of consumerism.

Section 47 of the Act allows for local authorities to carry out assessment in **such form** as the authority considers appropriate, for those who **may** be in need. This still leaves many consumers a long way from being empowered.

Needs-led assessment is far from easy and government guidance doesn't always help. Before assessment is undertaken, local authorities are advised to reach a decision, based on presenting need, of the level at which the assessment should be undertaken. This decision should be made by designated senior staff, but on what information?

The government tells us what kind of things to find out, above and beyond straightforward census data like name and address:

- Nature of the presenting problem
- Purpose of the intervention
- Urgency or risk
- Preferred solution
- Special requirements

from Practitioners' Guide, page 39

This is a clear Catch 22. By the time the allocation decision is made the assessment has already started: indeed, may even have finished! Neither are these simple pieces of information. That they may be gathered by the least well qualified staff builds additional danger into the process. This is serious in terms of human costs, and may also prove to be inefficient in financial terms. The increasing willingness of dissatisfied consumers in the Health Service to resort to litigation resulting in financial compensation will soon transfer to social services.

Nonetheless, current guidance is that people will be assessed by different levels of staff, according to an initial judgement about their likely needs. This runs as follows:

Assessment	Need	Staff
1 Simple	simple, defined	Reception or admin
2 Limited	limited, defined, low risk	Vocationally qualified
3 Multiple	range of limited, defined, low risk	Vocationally qualified or equivalent
4 Specialist a) simple	defined, specialist, low risk	Specialist ancillary
b) complex	ill-defined, complex, high risk	Specialist professional
5 Complex	ill-defined, inter-related, complex, volatile, high risk	Professionally qualified
6 Comprehensive	ill-defined, multiple, inter-related, high risk, severe	Professionally qualified and/or specialist professional
Practitioners' Guide p42		

This is clearly a nightmare to interpret both for consumers and staff. As stated earlier, there is a legal route straight to a comprehensive assessment for those adults who appear to be disabled under the terms of the 1986 Disabled Persons (SCR) Act. Taking this line does mean that a person should at least ensure their assessment is undertaken by someone professionally qualified.

Disability, like many legal categories, is open to interpretation, especially around words such as substantial, but it remains true that it is the stigmatic overtones of the word that prevent many people from classifying themselves as disabled rather than a rational judgement about their particular impairments.

Having decided who should be assessed and by whom, the next step is actually to do the business.

> *Disabled people are legally defined as persons aged 18 or over who are blind, deaf or dumb, or who suffer from mental disorder of any description and other persons aged 18 or over who are substantially and permanently handicapped by illness, injury, or congenital deformity.*
> **NHS & Community Care Act 1990**
>
> *A person has a disability... if he has a physical or mental impairment which has a substantial and long-term adverse effect on his ability to carry out normal day-to-day activities*
> **Disability Discrimination Act 1993**

THE FOLLOWING IS TAKEN FROM THE MANAGERS' GUIDE:

Assessing Need

Assessment Staff will, wherever possible, cease to be linked to specific services... The priority requirement for assessment staff will be an in-depth understanding of the needs associated with particular user groups and a knowledge of the range of services and community resources available to meet those needs...

> **In order to undertake an assessment of need, staff have to know:**
> - the needs for which the agency accepts responsibility
> - the needs for which other care agencies accept responsibiity
> - the needs of carers who qualify for assistance
> - the agency's priorities in responding to needs
> - the financial assessment criteria for determining users' contributions
> - the agency's policy on risk to the user and to the community
> - the legal requirements

Some social workers will smile at these requirements, since there is still far from universal agreement about who is responsible for what. The boundary between health and social services is still very muddy underfoot, as is that between the statutory and voluntary sector. Few agencies have established risk policies.

The Guide goes on to make it clear where responsibility lies for ensuring staff have the information they require, and to reinforce the policy of promoting a needs-led approach, which it seeks to reinforce by the use of revised proforma.

2.21 *It is the responsibility of management to ensure that this information is readily available to staff. It cannot be stressed enough that assessment of need must be distinguished from the care planning phase, to promote the needs-led approach. This differentiation should be reinforced by the way in which* **revised assessment proformas** *are drafted. For example, many existing proformas describe needs in terms of services. Needs are often professionally categorised in a way that fails to capture the desired outcome from the user's and /or carers' perspective.*

(Care Management and Assessment: Managers' Guide, p 46)

The Managers' Guide contains a number of models for managing assessment within the organisation, and there are clearly decisions to be reached around the cost-effective use of staff, particularly in the current climate of reducing the level of educational requirements to the most basic for workers conducting assessments, now regarded by many organisations as a stand-alone task. At the end of the day, however, the organisational model, or the title of the person conducting the assessment, will matter less to the person on the receiving end than their willingness to listen, and allow a participative model which respects their views and comes up with the goods. It may help if social workers were to conceptualise their role as coordinating the assessment **on behalf** of the individual, not controlling it.

The process of assessment is also available for us in government guidance. It makes it all sound very easy.

The aim is as follows:

● *'To understand an individual's needs; to relate them to agency policies and priorities, and to agree the objectives for any intervention.'*

This will strike those who believe in a user-centred assessment as a strange ordering for the aim, and it would have been more empowering had it read:

● '...*understand need, agree objectives, relate to policy and priority and then negotiate and agree services.*'

As it stands it implies that there is little point agreeing on any objectives unless they fit into agency policy, which brings us dangerously close to a service-led assessment. Much of the worth of any assessment for the potential service user will depend on the interpretation of the word 'relate' and the extent of any active negotiation or influence which the assessor can achieve within the organisation. It can mean little more than fitting an individual into pre-set eligibility criteria and pre-determined priorities.

The government goes on to recommend the following process in order to fulfil its aim:

- negotiate the scope of the assessment
- choose the setting
- clarify expectations
- promote partnership
- establish a relationship of trust
- assess need
- determine eligibility
- set priorities
- agree objectives
- record the assessment

Practitioners' Guide p47

This is not so simple as may appear at first glance, not least because the formula for meeting the original aim does not follow logically from it. The idea, for example, that you might go through the whole process from negotiating the scope of the assessment to assessing need and then find out that the person was ineligible for service has a nightmarish quality to it, and in practice it is inevitable that the decision about eligibility (or non eligibility) will be made early on and even before a worker is assigned the case. This is a resource-led decision and will suck the process down the line of being service-led unless organisations have very broad criteria which accept that everyone who is a child, is disabled, has mental health problems, or is vulnerable to personal or institutional abuse is eligible for service.

This brings the circle back to the logical conclusion that needs-led is only possible where there are adequate resources, because in any other environment many potential service users will be excluded from the system even **before** their needs are assessed and recorded. Resources here include not only the cost of any service resources which may be accessed as a result of the assessment process, but the resources to carry out the assessment in the first place. Assessments take time and cost money, and their numbers are consequently restricted by organisations.

So the first hurdle for the would-be consumer is getting themselves into the system. The next section takes a step back, and explores some of the age-old dynamics of need and demand, rationing and resource allocation.

The dynamics of need, demand and special need

This section aims to explore the concepts of need, demand and special need not as esoteric ideas but in the context of the more or less overt organisational agenda: how to distribute finite resources in the most equitable fashion. (More covert organisational agendas are discussed later). In doing so, it deliberately makes use of some old ideas such as rationing, deterrence and stigma, on the grounds that they more accurately represent reality for welfare service users than sanitised notions such as prioritisation or customer service.

> *'I need a holiday'*
>
> *'I need you, I need you, I need you...!'*

While much common speech uses 'need' as a verb, in welfare terms is it more usually a noun: indeed, as often as not with its own explanatory adjective. It is a pity that 'needs-led' has been set at the heart of community care, since it is fraught with the possibilities of misunderstanding. Hopes, wishes, aspirations, dreams and the barriers that prevent their realisation would have been so much easier to work with!

Need is at once a simple idea about which everyone has an understanding, (even if not necessarily a shared one) and a complex concept around which academic reputations are made. There is a huge and growing literature on the subject, and readers wishing to pursue the subject in depth are respectfully referred to their nearest university library. In the meantime, practitioners need some understanding with which to operate day to day.

The most enduring theory is that of Jonathan Bradshaw, whose article in *New Society* in March 1972 – much quoted and little read – set a useful baseline for an understanding of need in a social welfare context. He gave us four varieties. (See box page 23) Time moves on. We now have such concepts as 'universal need' which envisages some basic cross-cultural commonality; and 'real need' (or 'the professional knows best') which can be utilised by those in power to override the wishes of those who are less powerful. The notion of 'special need' is clearly discriminatory, yet it is a concept which few have chosen to challenge.

Needs can even be counted. It is not unusual nowadays to read documents or research reports which add up the number of **needs**, make comparisons between people on that basis, or make the case for additional resources on the basis of unmet needs.

The idea that human need can be quantified in such a way may be music to the ears of auditors or those compiling charts to illustrate research reports, but it is an over simplification. Without some agreement about what constitutes **a need**, met or unmet, such figures have little usefulness and there is little point in recording them.

What may be more useful indicators to those seeking to provide help would be to record barriers to achievement, shortfalls in provision or the outcome of assessments which result in recommendations for mainstream facilities such as libraries, leisure centres, playgroups and so on that are often denied to whole sections of the community because of race, disability, class or poverty. The difficulty is that gaining such information means entering a process which raises expectations, and which encourages people to ask for resources. Cash-strapped organisations who are legally obliged to provide free or subsidised services don't like doing this!

Despite the dictates of legislation to be proactive and inform people of their rights, public service departments are not in the business of encouraging people to express their desires or aspirations, especially where there is no matching service. The purchaser/provider split is intended to address this by separating the assessment for service from its provision, but the processes by which people express their need are not simple.

At a basic level a thirsty man is likely to frame his desire in terms of what is available, known to him or preferable as a means of meeting his need: maybe a pint of beer or a mug of tea. When a woman goes looking for a new outfit her need may be for something to give her confidence, but she is not conditioned to express her demand in that way in the shop. The individual who goes to a buy a bigger car is unlikely to tell the salesman he needs to feel more powerful. If in such day-to-day examples needs-led has become service led, how much more complex will it be when a whole lifestyle is under discussion?

Both health and social welfare service provision may be perceived as stigmatic, which may deter applicants. But even allowing for that there is still many a slip between the dry lip and the cup which prevents those who could benefit, from receiving public service. Decisions about who receives and who is denied service are not made by individual consumers, unless you include the prerogative to refuse an offer, but by organisations on the basis of sets of information about the service user on the one hand and a 'knowledge' of the organisation's priorities and resources on the other. Ignorance by either the potential service user or the organisational representative can create mismatch. Worse, there is often no realisation by either party that there is a misunderstanding. Social services believe that their information is good, while the potential consumers believe that they know what kind of services are available, and what sort of people get them.

Resource allocation decisions at all levels are often made behind closed doors, and behind the protective curtain of 'confidentiality'. When these decisions involve the allocation of resources such as sheltered housing flats or residential places to one applicant at the expense of another, ostensibly on the basis of the most needy, they leave little time for anyone to question the decision nor any clear grounds on which to do so.

Rationing is nonetheless necessary where resources are limited and are indivisible. It is feasible to manage cuts in education by increasing class size, for example, but a sheltered housing flat cannot be allocated on a timeshare basis in order to be fair to all the applicants. The equitable allocation of finite and often indivisible resources is the conundrum with which all public welfare services have to wrestle.

Different political and ideological perspectives will propose different approaches. The marketplace philosophy would lead neatly into allocation on the basis of ability to pay and the British culture into a first come, first served, queuing system. The new Right would endorse a rigorous policy of deterrence, while insisting at the same time on citizens' rights and charters. There are elements of all these systems within the various processes which welfare organisations have devised to deliver services, but the reality is more complex than any of them.

Demand can be reduced by a variety of means. Ignorance has been mentioned, and stigma will be explored later. Charging for service is an obvious deterrent, as is the arduous form filling which passes for assessment in some organisations.

However, the restriction of demand, as opposed to supply, may work against the wish of the organisation to maximise its resources. Organisations interested in increasing their resources may wish to inflate overt demand to demonstrate their popularity to grant-awarding bodies, lottery committees, housing corporations or government departments. Organisations do this by such devices as long waiting lists and the rigorous collection and recording of 'unmet need'. Playing the system like this can lead to distorted pictures of what is actually required in service terms.

This can be benign in service user terms, but it may mean the unkind raising of expectations. The housing association which was the subject of my PhD thesis maintained a 'waiting list' of 20 people for every available place, in order to demonstrate demand for the resource.

It should not be assumed that there is a simple split between the rationing organisation and the grasping consumer. Consumers of health and welfare are bombarded with the message of cuts, and understand that resources are limited and that choices have to be made. Some consumers are inevitably more altruistic than others so that some equitable and independent means of making such choices has to be found. People are more likely to be discontented by rationing when it perceived as unfair, or when the method of resource allocation is hidden.

NEED — a brief commentary based on Jonathan Bradshaw's theory

Bradshaw suggested there are four different ways of defining need: normative, felt, expressed and comparative.

Normative need is that decided on by the professional, expert or administrator on behalf of the community at large. The professional works on some desirable standard. The two principle ways would be to aim at a minimum standard, or to aim at an ideal. In practice, welfare systems go for the minimum standard, or safety net. Beveridge hoped to lay down minimum standards when he helped devise the concept of the welfare state. The problem with such a system is that there is no incentive for its operators to rise above the minimum so that, in practice, floors have a tendency to become ceilings.

Felt needs, which Bradshaw equated with want, are limited or enhanced by the perceptions, knowledge and experience of the individual.

Expressed needs are felt needs actually translated into a demand for service. A person is, however, likely only to express demands they feel are likely to be met; are not too stigmatic; or where there is nothing to lose in the attempt. Demand is, therefore, an inaccurate measure of felt need.

Comparative need is arrived at by a comparison of two areas of need with each other in terms of services available to similar groups, areas or individuals. The gap between them is comparative need. This approach can be used in an attempt to standardise provision, but may not relate to need. The fact that one area is better serviced than the next does not mean it is adequately served.

SPECIAL NEEDS

Jonathan Bradshaw did not include special needs in his theory. Indeed, most academic theorists do not, but the invention and the persistence of the category in social policy hives off certain groups of people from mainstream assessment and provision, less for their own benefit than to maintain the quality of provision for those who are not special. It is a pernicious categorisation, not least because it is couched in language which pretends to be benign. One group particularly disadvantaged in this way are disabled children. Increasingly, children who are disruptive in school are being classed as having special needs, with recommendations that they are educated separately.

The basic needs of disabled children are no different from those of any other children. All children need (or have a right to) warmth, security, food, to be loved, to play, to learn, to grow, to take risks, to make friends and explore relationships, and to be free from abuse and exploitation. The concept of 'special need' has been extremely misleading in promoting a notion that disabled children somehow have different needs from the rest of children. What is different is the barriers which relate specifically to disabled children, and make them 'special'. Alternatively, the usual means of meeting the need which is appropriate to non-disabled children may not help a child with a particular impairment. Disability is made worse for some children by the absence of appropriate artificial aids. For example when being fed, a disabled child may simply require a spoon of a different shape or made from different material. If this is available, the disability may disappear or become merely an inconvenience. It is worth remembering that many widely used artificial aids are not considered stigmatic, nor their users considered to be disabled because of reliance on them: glasses for short sight are an obvious example, but we might also cite toothbrushes, forks or light bulbs.

In weighing options against each other for meeting needs, or securing rights, social workers should be mindful of the normal ways of meeting them, within whatever family or cultural setting, and then try to ascertain why that solution is not available for the particular disabled child.

Some of these difficulties are more intractable than others, but the stock responses of isolated, adult-oriented play at home, or special day care, will not fulfil the child's need to experience a normal childhood. Nor is the current fad for providing sound and light rooms for severely disabled children and adults any substitute for a trip to the park, although I suspect that such developments are prefiguring a trend toward the virtual reality of the holo-suite which lies in store for all of us.

An assessment relating to a disabled child should not

focus on the deficiency of the child, but on the barriers to their hopes and aspirations, within their own context. It follows that any assessment must start with the aim of finding out what these hopes and aspirations might be. Funnily enough, this is the same good practice as an assessment for any other child, or for an adult for that matter. There is nothing special about it.

The reasons for maintaining the illusion of special needs are a combination of organisational requirements to ration and an enduring societal fear of children and adults who are different. Both are vicious circles.

STIGMA

Originally, assessment related to taxation and was the process by which the amount owing was fixed. It is perhaps this unpleasant meaning which has infiltrated our collective subconscious and made us wary. Assessment is certainly not something that occurs when things are going well, and in welfare terms seems to be a process that visits marginalised groups of the population rather more than it does those in the mainstream of society. As such, it is less associated with gaining rights than identifying problems.

The deterrent practices of many social services departments do little to alter these perceptions. This is all common knowledge, but has to remain on our agendas until things change.

Deterrence: 20 ways to minimise demand!

1. Onerous and complicated application forms
2. Hard-to-find offices
3. Inaccessible buildings
4. Poor sign-posting
5. All white staff in a multi-racial area
6. Overbooking, failure to stick to appointment times, or broken promises to visit
7. Long queues, or waiting times for home visits
8. Poorly equipped waiting rooms, or waiting in corridors
9. Inadequate toilet facilities
10. Nowhere to feed or change a baby
11. Unfriendly reception staff
12. Opaque panels at reception
13. Cold and uncomfortable interviewing rooms
14. Hurried interviews
15. Lack of privacy for interviewing
16. Charging policies
17. Lack of information
18. Poor reputation
19. Unsympathetic attitude of professional staff
20. Registration

Deterrent practices are sometimes justified by the adage that only the really desperate will negotiate them. In practice, it is more likely to be the most confident. Professionals act both as gatekeepers for their organisations and as brokers or advocates to access the services of others. In both cases, it may be seen that needing the recommendation of a social worker carries its own stigma. The service is not available as of right, but only if the social worker is prepared to grant it.

This process can deny the right to people to be experts about their own needs. It is a particular issue for the disability movement, which argues that disabled people are undermined by social services, medicine and charitable institutions all of which deny that disabled people are autonomous and independent individuals who can make their own choices about lifestyle. Disabled adults are systematically excluded from employment opportunities, just as disabled children are excluded from mainstream education. Both processes are fed by the belief that disabled people are inadequate and a drain on society's resources. As such, assessments are often focused on the needs of the carer or the local community rather than the disabled person. There has been a sad exchange between the interests of carers and the interests of disabled people in recent years, which has diverted the energies of both away from the real issues of the exploitative system which expects relatives to act as personal attendants, regardless of the wishes of the disabled person, or of their own wishes.

The control over lifestyle is denied to many disabled people partly in an attempt to conserve resources, but also because large sections of the population have no wish to include disabled people as equals. Readers will be familiar with the NIMBY phenomenon which involves local residents in resisting developments such as mental health hostels or homes for people with learning disabilities being opened in their own back yards. Charlie Brown's assertion that he loves humanity, but cannot stand people, seems to apply particularly when some people are deemed more desirable neighbours than others. No one wants unpleasant or antisocial neighbours, but the vigour which drives these campaigns is not based on knowledge of particular individuals, but on prejudice about certain groups of the population. Issues around disablism are fully discussed in a number of other books in this series.

Professionals wishing to break into these vicious circles of stigma and deterrence in order to help people get the best out of the system have to tackle it on a number of fronts.

Something has to be done to tackle the issues on the list of deterrents. Some of this will cost money.

The provision of information about services and the means of accessing them is a legal requirement, and improving the quality of that information and the means of its dissemination is a necessary prerequisite to enabling people to make better use of the services available. Providing accurate and accessible information may well increase demand, but it should also mean it is more accurately directed. Given adequate information, many people will be able to make more appropriate requests for service and many will become self-servicing: if the organisation will let them!

Those who prefer to seek professional advice should be free to do so. A change of language from that prescribed by the government might help. Assessments could be framed in terms of aspirations and identifying the means to achieve them, rather than in terms of needs and services. Social workers could reasonably act as a bridge for people to access mainstream advice about education, employment, leisure, finance, health care, legal services, housing and transport. For some people this may entail bridging a gap in personal confidence or life experience. In other cases, it may involve the worker acting on the individual's behalf to convince the employer, head teacher, leisure centre manager or financial adviser that the disabled person will not embarrass him or eat his children. In other cases it may involve the worker convincing the individual that other disabled people have been in the same position and can help.

A similar philosophy can be adopted for other groups of potential service users. After all the above have been explored with or by the individual concerned, the best chance of attaining or retaining the preferred lifestyle may be the provision of services from the local authority, voluntary organisation or through contracted private sector provision. The key factor in eliminating stigma is less how aspirations are met than how much control the individual has over the process and the outcome.

This means professionals walking a tightrope between, on the one hand, giving advice and information based on their own knowledge and experience, and on the other taking over as experts. It is a balancing act which sometimes requires very keen antennae.

The alert reader will have noticed that I have now advocated both juggling and tightrope walking as essential skills for a good assessor. The circus has frequently struck me as a pertinent analogy for the social services, in which social workers are cast as the high wire acrobats, operating with or without a safety net. It is dangerous to get too caught up in analogies, so I will respectfully leave the fun of allocating the roles of ringmaster, human cannonball, lions and lion tamers, knifethrowers... and clowns, of course... to your own imaginations!

Organisational agendas

It is clear from the efforts made to devise and introduce assessment forms, procedures and dedicated staff that assessment is an organisationally valued activity. However, it would be naïve not to acknowledge that the agendas of those organisations may not always match those of the professionals within them – nor those of their service users. Professionals, or others undertaking assessments, must understand this mismatch because they are the brokers of information.

Holding up hands in dismay and despair does not help: it is incumbent on the professional not only to seek to influence the organisation within which they work, but to manage the mismatch as effectively as they can to ensure the best deal for the potential service user. This dynamic gets even more complicated where assessments are multi disciplinary, and assessors have to work with the agendas of more than one organisation.

Given these complexities, it is foolish to pretend that any of this is easy. Good assessment should be undertaken by experienced and skilled staff, with the understanding of and ability to work within the organisational context. The assessor is both representing the organisation to the person being assessed, and translating their views back to the organisation.

In this latter sense, there is something of the advocate in the role, although it is arguable that someone who is employed by an organisation cannot reasonably be expected to act as an advocate. Indeed, and while not wishing to indulge in too cynical a discourse on welfare organisations, it is possible that some employers would prefer the assessor simply to represent the interests of the organisation, in which case the ill-educated but well-trained company automaton will serve their purpose. The fragmentation of social work into its constituent functional tasks is fuelling fears that workers' ability to see past their own immediate tasks will disintegrate.

There are strong voices which argue that advocacy must be independent of the organisations which assess and allocate resources. It is a model which has the attraction of simplicity and logic, and it informs the theory behind the purchaser/provider split. It appeals both to independent advocates and to those employers who prefer staff who ask few questions. The difficulty is that it assists the process of fragmentation, and encourages welfare organisations not to employ the sort of professional who can see both sides of the picture, which will ultimately disadvantage the interests of service users. Advocacy remains a key role for social workers, despite the obvious constraints imposed by the employer/employee relationship.

This section explores the reasons why organisations assess, apart from the wholly straightforward goal of seeking to find out what it is their service users require. While this uncomplicated aim remains at the centre of their policy, what follows suggests that there are other forces at work. Additional agendas are concerned with bureaucratic demands; the use of resources and their internal distribution; the rationing of scarce resources; and public accountability. All of these pressures impinge on the assessment process.

PUBLIC ACCOUNTABILITY: THE AUDIT TRAIL OR JUSTIFYING EXPENDITURE

Being publicly accountable is not quite the same as being a careful housekeeper. The emphasis is not so much on being careful about how money is spent or resources allocated, which few would argue with as essential in public bodies, but on the means adopted **to be seen to be** being careful.

Auditors and inspectors want to see solid evidence of systems, within which there must be logical and formula-based outcomes for set inputs. Auditors, chairs of complaints panels and judicial reviewers tend not to like matters left to individual circumstance, professional judgement or negotiation. Rather they are interested in set criteria and written rules. Impressive-looking assessment tools may not assist the analytical process one jot, but they are valued as evidence that something scientific is going on. As long as the system looks equitable, it can very reasonably be used by the organisation to justify rationing.

Organisations do not want to be told that what passes as rational criteria depends very much on the value judgements of the individual ticking the boxes, and even on the time of day the assessment was performed.

TO ASSIST RATIONING

Not only can pseudo-scientific assessment tools be used to justify rationing, they act as rationing devices in themselves: they put people off. Social workers who get to someone's house, open a bulging briefcase and produce a large form dehumanise the process and keep control a long way from the service user, and incidentally, from themselves. Social workers who are interested in the promotion of the rights of individuals face a very real dilemma when asked to act as rationers of service, since their professional judgement will almost certainly conflict with the role placed on them by the organisation. Small wonder that authorities seeking to limit expenditure are tempted to employ unqualified staff to conduct assessments of need. This is supported by government guidance which suggests that 'simple' assessments or those where there is low risk do not require professionally qualified assessors. **(See p14)**

COMPARATIVE DATA

Once completed, standardised assessment forms can be used by the organisation to compare resource allocation across different professionals, or area offices, and so rule out idiosyncratic behaviour. This can lead to performance-related pay based, not on consumer views about the standard of service from an individual, but on countable criteria such as number of assessments completed, and the time taken to complete them. Such nonsense affects other services such as the police, probation and community nursing. The number of arrests is more profitable for an aspiring officer than crime prevention; probation officers are measured by the time they take to compile a court report, not the quality of its content, and nurses by the number of visits made, not by the quality of treatment.

BUREAUCRATIC CONTROL V. PROFESSIONAL JUDGEMENT

A creeping madness is currently affecting medicine, in which doctors are at growing risk of being sued not so much for negligence, which is reasonable, but for making the wrong decision about treatment. Medicine is based as much on intelligent guesswork and experience as it is on pure science, and the effect of the growth in solicitor-driven litigation is either to drive doctors towards opting for the safe option (for them) or to avoid sharing speculations with patients. This defensive medicine has resulted, for example, in a growth in the number of babies born by Caesarean sections. What lies behind this is a growing belief in the ultimate scientific rationality of medicine as a process, which will render human judgement unnecessary. A similarly dangerous belief is entering social work, with a tendency towards educating people less and relying instead on paper or computer-based systems to make sense of the complexity of human experience.

Many managers would prefer a system for resource allocation which did not rely on professional judgement, and encourage the development of clever forms or assessment tools instead. There may be some attraction in the fact that a form, unlike an individual, cannot be sued. It takes a confident person to become a doctor or a social worker these days, and every social worker knows that bureaucracy can be both friend and foe. It serves both to provide a structure within which to make sense of the often complex processes of people's lives but also, on the negative side, handicaps and impedes by an insistence on set procedures. Bureaucracy is one means by which an organisation controls and restricts the activities of its staff, and its restrictive effects are inevitably felt the more keenly by those who seek to work creatively or speedily.

To put it another way: professionals are disempowered by being hedged in by bureaucratic hurdles, rules and criteria. Worse, some workers are more likely to encounter such difficulties than others.

It is a fact of institutional life that some individuals are allowed to sail closer to the wind than others. Institutional racism or sexism operates not so much by having different rules for black people or women, but by insisting on the letter of the law in their case, while allowing the in-crowd to bend or break it. By its very nature the evidence for such practice is anecdotal, but the case of Alison Halford versus Merseyside Police is one very clear example of a woman being penalised for behaviour that would go unremarked in a man. **(Halford 1993)** More general examples include dress codes.

A similar dynamic operates to control professionals who advocate too strongly for their clients. Thus a strong advocate for a service user who wants something different can be disempowered simply by the invocation of a rule that might otherwise lie unused. Social workers trying to do something unusual will be constantly stymied by someone who knows what is written in paragraph 63, subsection c, bracket ii. It is hard to know how to challenge such controlling systems, and a great many people simply give in and learn to play by the book. As a matter of survival (and no-one changes a system unless they survive) it is important to identify allies and be clear enough about political or managerial agendas to know when it is likely to be worth making a stand. Inevitably, perhaps, professional and managerial interests will differ and have to be constantly re-negotiated.

ORGANISATIONAL AGENDAS: POLITICS

Welfare organisations seem sometimes to be working against the ability of their own professional staff to act in the best interests of their consumers. There are pressures on professionals to recommend the services of their own organisations, or those with whom the authority has contractual arrangements.

Public sector organisations have to serve political masters which may act against their being supportive environments for the delivery of effective welfare. In the 1990s in particular, the political agenda has espoused self help which means being seen to be tough on scroungers or those who do not take responsibility for themselves or for their families. It is a climate of self-sufficiency and the survival of the fittest.

Local authorities are not built up from local need, but are essentially devices for the distribution of monies made available by central government, whether it is redistributed from national taxation or collected locally according to rules laid down by the centre. Standard Spending Assessments introduced in 1990 are calculated centrally on population estimates and deprivation factors. The auditors are very much in the driving seat, which strengthens a managerial, rather than a professional culture.

A further cloud which is looming determinedly on the horizon is political uncertainty, under which Community Care and the Children Act were introduced and continue to operate. Conservative governments seek to limit the power of local authorities, and officers in Labour-controlled councils in particular experience considerable tension trying to balance the demands of central and local politicians. Local authorities are struggling to survive: arguably this is no time to rock the boat.

The almost contemporaneous introduction of the NHS & Community Care Act and the Children Act brought with it competing philosophies and demands, and the threat or opportunity of restructuring. These organisational changes tended to be from the top down, and to be introduced in haste, although some authorities were a great deal sooner off the mark than others. Typically, they did not start by devising systems for exploring user need, by whatever definition, nor consult local people about their preferences. The first phase was invariably to change the management structure; then to deploy staff and develop criteria to allocate resources.

ORGANISATIONAL AGENDAS: TURF WARS

The previous discussions are written on the assumption that the organisational agenda is synonymous with that of its management, but different from that of its professional staff. The reality is more complex. As well as the management/professional tension, there will be issues arising from restructuring, internal power struggles and personal and sectional ambitions. There is nothing peculiar to welfare organisations in all this.

Within most large organisations, there is an internally-driven resource war between differing budget holders, each conditioned to maximise the size of their own empire, because its size is related to status, income, career and power: all of which are usually more convincing motivators than corporate responsibility.

While redistributing resources might mean better services for users and internal change can be for the better, internal competition as the process which drives change suits some organisations better than others. Those with growing external sources of income, or those chasing new markets will wish to encourage it as it will result in overall growth. In the climate of limited overall resources which characterises both state welfare and voluntary organisations any increase in the size of one assistant director's sphere of influence is necessarily at the expense of another. It is often the better game-players who win at the expense of an independent or dispassionate study of how best to deliver services to a given geographical area.

Social services have become bedevilled by turf wars during the 1990s. These have been between the more ancient contenders of childcare and adults on the one hand, and between the new groupings of purchasers and providers on the other. In the growing patterns of schism within organisations, everyone becomes a customer of someone else and – despite the ideal of a seamless service – it is increasingly impossible for consumers to know who is responsible for what. The internal recharge has become a way of life in a culture where everything, including advice, has its price.

This is not confined to social services, of course, but is an ideologically-driven confusion affecting many public services, and ex-public services. The old Gas Board is now three companies, at least. One owns the gas, another the meter, and a third has the maintenance contracts.

This kind of activity can skew assessments in a number of ways. Service providers want customers, and of the right type, particularly if faced with external competition. They may wish to demonstrate the need for service by inflating demand, keeping long waiting lists or convincing people through the use of scare tactics that not using the service is bad for their health. Professionals attempting to help disabled people set up home in the community will be familiar with providers of institutional care or respite who will invoke worst case scenarios to frighten parents, relatives and councillors into the safe option. Service providers are dependent on purchasers for much of their custom, but many purchasers are unable to specify what it is they wish to buy because they lack detailed knowledge and expertise. Those organisations with expertise in marketing are increasingly likely to get the contracts, given the paucity of objective measures of the quality of their service. This puts the relatively ignorant purchaser in much the same position as the non mechanically-minded seeking to buy a used car. What is worse, is that he is purchasing not to meet his own needs, but those of an even more hapless service user.

There is also a danger of organisationally-driven invocation of expertise to maintain control of access to certain resources, where some 'assessments' can only be made, say, by an occupational therapist or member of a specialist team. This is a difficult area, in that these professionals do have areas of expertise and develop experience, but where this becomes a tool for ring fencing resources within divisions or specialist teams it becomes unhelpful. It is also an area where professional preciousness can work with new managerialism to disempower service users.

INTER-ORGANISATIONAL AGENDAS

Turf wars are not confined to the internal struggles of agencies. Resource-strapped local authorities and health authorities are engaged in depressing and time-consuming demarcation disputes. There are growing cultural differences between local authority councillors and the non-elected boards of health authorities and trusts. Much of the demarcation debate is political rather than professional, since most professionals recognise that the needs of people for community care do not fall neatly into either a social or a health category. This recognition has not prevented the kind of professional distrust which saw, for example, community occupational therapists refusing to accept the recommendations of those based in hospital.

What is depressing is the relish with which many people in health and social services have embraced and enacted these idiocies in public service, together with the trappings and jargon of new managerialism that go along with it. The existence of so much strife does not bode well for inter agency co-operation. Happily the indications are that professionals in health, social care and education are becoming more disillusioned with their own organisations, and for similar reasons, than they are interested in continuing inter-professional rivalry. To be idealistic just for a minute, there are still enough people, despite all this organisational chaos, who are interested in providing a competent and ethical service and in doing their own job well. It is through such people that change has to come, but the inter-agency agenda cannot be left to individual good-will. Effective inter-agency working is essential for the effective delivery of community care.

Inter-agency working

This is a huge topic, and much of its heartache has focused on the increasingly arid debate around the boundary between health and social care.

This is a politically driven argument and not one I wish to spend much time on here. The following therefore skims over the surface of the community care conundrums, and moves to consider inter-agency and inter-professional concerns at the assessment level. In particular it looks at what happens in all this fluidity, conflict and change to 'people who don't fit' into the systems because they have both health and social care needs or because they cross the service user groups. They are often people with complex needs, who are a risk to themselves and others, but the 'impossible client' may also be a creation of the bureaucratic divisions. Challenging behaviour may mean those whose behaviour challenges the system!

The introduction of care in the community requires more sophisticated collaborative arrangements than hospital or institutional delivery of services. The medical model, based on ordering treatments, does not sit very comfortably with a collaborative approach, which means the traditional GP is a poor foundation on which to build. With the move away from specialist hospital care to the more generalist primary health care team as the focus of provision it is nonetheless on the GP that prime responsibility as a broker of services will increasingly fall. This will create inevitable tension between the GP as medical practitioner and the new role of the GP as small business manager. At the moment, GPs often leave both the treatment and management of some groups of patients to other specialist services. Many people with mental health problems, learning disability or physical impairment have in the past not been dealt with by the GP. Moving into this area of responsibility as purchasers in the primary care system may not be a progressive move. While such people should have access to their GP for **medical** problems, on the same basis as anyone else who falls ill, it is debatable whether there is any advantage in GPs undertaking community care responsibilities on any wider basis. Much of what people require to maintain themselves in the community is not medically based.

In reality, most mental health problems relate to such issues as housing, finance, stress at work, unemployment or inter-personal relationships, all of which are social issues. Despite this obvious fact, government guidance puts the medical agenda at the heart of the collaborative venture **(Building Bridges DOH 1995).** It urges training for other disciplines which starts with the causes and symptoms of major mental disorders, and it sets the medically-led Care Programme approach as the cornerstone of mental health services. Social services departments charged with purchasing and providing services for mentally ill people living in the community, and with providing Approved Social Workers to undertake emergency assessments have somehow to fit their care management around the prescriptive statutory duties imposed by Mental Health legislation. Good practice means moving people out of locked institutions and into the community, but without either adequate resources or widespread support for the policy.

Many of the current working practices for inter-agency collaboration are derived from a continuum model based around hospital discharge planning. While this will continue, it is increasingly nonsensical to expect that people in need of community care services will have to go into hospital to access the system, or indeed, even to get ill.

Despite the emphasis on continuing care, the hospital-based providers will continue to exercise considerable influence, even where the problems are no longer acute. The ascendency of the medical model dictates the pattern for services for people with mental health problems well beyond the asylum walls. The power of the psychiatrist in the multidisciplinary team makes individual pathology and drug-based regimes normal models of practice, and compulsory detention of mentally ill people an acceptable model of practice. Dependency on prescribed drugs is socially acceptable, provided one is willing to accept the label of mental ill health, but they have no more power to solve the underlying problems than alcohol or cigarettes, and carry similar disadvantages. Drug dependency, provided the drugs are legal, is encouraged by government because the alternative would be to acknowledge that society places intolerable pressures on vast numbers of people.

Change entails developing models for practice which are entirely community based, and which do not rely on a medical lead. Much work in the field of adult disability is driven by the imperative from the disability movement not to confuse disability and ill health. This movement has led to some progress in thinking about ways to ensure adequate access for all to mainstream provision, regardless of physical impairment. Such things as housing, education and employment are currently denied to many people because of such things as inaccessible buildings, the organisation of lessons or the prejudice of employers. Sometimes called the social model, this seeks to replace such pathologising thinking with an alternative which argues that disabled people are denied full citizenship on the basis of difference.

Exclusion affects many groups such as members of minority ethnic communities for whom the whiteness of health and welfare presents a major barrier, and gays and lesbians who continue to experience deep-seated ignorance and prejudice from medical, health care and social welfare professionals.

MULTI-DISCIPLINARY ASSESSMENT

The Department of Health may be driving a move toward community, and therefore more generalist, health care in an effort to end the stranglehold of hospital consultants, but overall professional and organisational boundaries are not dissolving so much as re-forming. New professional roles and titles are emerging. The primary health care team now has an enormous and growing range of allied professions. The free market is developing an increasing variety of forms of complementary medicine as people refuse to accept the limitations of traditional western practice. The shifts into a market-led health and social care economy mean local authorities are charged with encouraging private and voluntary provision, each with their own criteria and target client group. Add to this the enormous number of Health Care Trusts who have carved up the old NHS and the problem becomes increasingly mind-blowing.

Multi-disciplinary assessment trips nicely off the tongue as a panacea in these confused times, but its dangers are still very real. It is based on the comfortable but unproven assumption that two or more heads are better than one but is often repetitive and complicated by differing organisational agendas and ethos, which then have to be disentangled. Many people caught into the assessment game will find themselves asked the same questions over and over again by professionals who have not learned to trust each other nor to share information on an equitable basis. Confidentiality is more usually invoked by professionals to protect their areas, than by patients, clients, or customers who normally expect that professionals who refer cases will talk to each other.

While there are instances when specialist knowledge is necessary to add to the picture of someone's situation, it is often debatable how many people really should get involved. The fundamental problems around multi-disciplinary work are duplication and fudged responsibility, so that consumers are frequently utterly confused about who does what. The way forward is not to introduce more professionals into the picture, nor is it to introduce a key worker as an additional player, but to ensure through adequate education and training that the person employed to undertake the assessment is competent.

In some areas attempts have been made to legitimise the assessments made by staff of one agency, such as community nurses, to access resources of another, such as social services. This kind of initiative largely foundered, not so much because nurses and social workers failed to respect each other's judgements, although that is part of it, but because managers in both organisations were never able to delegate enough responsibility in budget terms to empower their own staff, let alone anyone else's.

A more workable model is that of jointly employing assessors. Such individuals need a full appreciation of service possibilities across agencies. The danger of becoming service-led is still very real, and the success of such schemes in terms of the quality of service to the individual will depend very much on the level of training such individuals receive, and how far they can retain independence of vision from their employing agencies.

Case conferences were used as a means of inter-agency decision-making long before community care was heard of. They may have progressed over the years from professional get-togethers, to meetings the subject was invited to attend, to those where the individual concerned was invited to chair the meeting, but none of this disguises their essential artificially as an arena for making life-planning decisions, as opposed to making such decisions work in practice.

The case conference model is only used on a regular basis for those individuals who are caught into the social or health care system. Most people arrive at such conclusions about their lives in a less pressured and public way, over a longer time scale and in conjunction with confidantes of their own choosing.

Inter-agency meetings of such scale are of dubious value for individual assessment purposes although they may be more effective as means of agreeing service priorities, responsibilities and prices, which are managerial as much as professional decisions.

These tensions and strains are highlighted when health and social care professionals are asked to deal with the increasing number of individuals who do not fit into society's norm. These are the people who challenge the structures, processes and procedures by falling into the increasing number of holes created in the health/social care fabric. Some things are very clear, all the same. Those customers who are the most awkward to manage are still the most likely to be left on the doorstep of the statutory agencies at the end of the day.

Holes in the fabric (or along the continuum if you like) are created, ironically, by the growing emphasis on protocols, eligibility criteria and targeted services, but it is not a new phenomenon. In an article in *Health Trends* in 1983, Ruth Eley and I described how attempts to fit people into narrowly defined specialist service provision resulted in problems of allocation of resources.

The change in emphasis from institutional to community care means only that the care continuum has shifted from being building-based to professional- or person-based. Services are now based on the levels of assessment and status of the professional involved. In social services this is around care assistants, social workers, ASWs and care managers. In the primary health care team the continuum runs hierarchically through practice nurses; specialist practice nurses; nurse practitioners, general practitioners and specialist general practitioners, as well as a range of professions allied to medicine. The Care Programme approach for people with mental health problems is tiered from 'minimal' through 'more complex' to 'full, multi-disciplinary CPA' for those who represent significant risk.

> **Every time more specialised provision is introduced into the care continuum at least three things follow:**
> - A more sophisticated selection technique has to be devised to meet narrowed criteria of eligibility
> - More gaps are left for people to fall through
> - A person whose circumstances change, for better or worse, is more likely to find himself under pressure to move elsewhere
>
> *(Eley and Middleton 1983)*

This pattern creates the same issues of eligibility criteria, priority setting, opportunities for playing off, and gaps to fall through, that Ruth Eley and I highlighted over ten years ago in institutional terms. The important decision for patients or clients about who does their assessment, or whether they see anyone at all, is likely to be made by a receptionist or by the patients themselves. Access to information is crucial and yet few people probably understand the complexities of health and social services well enough to get the best for themselves. The panacea seems to be the production of leaflets, although there is little evidence that anyone reads or digests information in such a form, whatever language they are produced in. People who do understand may play the system in their own interests: it pays in terms of obtaining

a higher-ranking assessor to overplay symptoms and
problems from the outset, since that is when eligibility
decisions are made.

Those people who wish to command attention will
display challenging behaviour of one kind or another,
because the system encourages such attention seeking.
The system thus encourages dependency and the
medicalisation of situations: ironically, quite the opposite
of what government has in mind for the self-sufficient
society.

The way out of the complex service provisions issue is
beyond the scope of this book, but suffice to say, the
answer is the same as it always was, idealistic or not:
People need good standard housing and income levels,
backed up by flexible services that are not tied to
institutions.

The problem of over-assessment, fudged and dodged
responsibilities, and wasted resources between agencies, is
something that should be solved when organisations are
mature enough to work together. This may or may not
mean trust, but it will have to mean reaching negotiated
agreements which are mutually acceptable.

Good and bad assessment

Everyone interprets assessment differently. For some it has acquired a certain grandeur and become part of the toolbag of professional mystique. These are the sort of individuals most likely to arrive with huge assessment documents, or laptop computers, collect and record masses of data, do mysterious calculations with it, assign people scores, and behave as if something scientific was going on. They will have the backing of the auditors in this activity, if only because the auditors need to believe that assessment is somehow a scientific process. That means that the same result or score would be achieved if the process was repeated the next day, and the next, and the next. Nothing so simple.

The belief that there is some way of effectively and consistently measuring Case A with Case B in terms of their need for resources is attractive to those who have to justify rationing, but it is essentially illusive. Humanity is too complex, and the real skill is not in achieving a measuring tool or set of tools that fits everyone, but in being able to reach an accommodation with individuals which best fits their aspirations and the resources that can be made available. This is much harder in itself. Neither does it avoid the inevitable necessity to justify decisions to all parties. It is therefore unsurprising in a culture which seeks to blame rather than support that many workers have so willingly embraced the easy option of the pseudo-scientific assessment tool which only requires them to tick boxes and do a little simple arithmetic.

For ease of reading I have used the term 'the individual' throughout the next section, although the assessment could equally well be about the situation of a family, couple, child or carer. This is shorthand for the more accurate 'the individual whose situation is being assessed' which seems clumsy, and was chosen in preference to the more popular 'service user', because not all assessments will result in service provision. I have also used 'she' in preference to 'he', not simply out of perversity, but because I believe it conjures up a different image. Most service users, including carers, and most social workers, are women, after all.

THE PROCESS OF ASSESSMENT

THE PROCESS OF ASSESSMENT

1 Establishing a working relationship
- i   timing it
- ii   establishing groundrules
- iii   acknowledging feelings

2 Data collection
- i   aspirations: what the individual wants
- ii   barriers/problems/stresses
- iii   resources/sources of support
- iv   coping mechanisms
- v   expert evidence

3 Analysis
- i   what the individual wants
- ii   identifying changes which are required
- iii   identifying risks
- iv   identifying opportunities
- v   identifying the role of service providers
- vi   costing
- vii   weighing up the options

4 Planning
- i   draft proposals
- ii   negotiation
- iii   recommendations
- iv   arrangements for review
- v   ensuring quality

A good assessment is a logical process, and will follow more or less the pattern which follows, although there will be inevitable loops forward and backwards through the list:

STAGE ONE: ESTABLISHING A WORKING RELATIONSHIP

A great deal is made in social work about the value of establishing and maintaining good relationships with people, and while this is an undeniable prerequisite of useful work, there is often far too much mystique and preciousness about it. It is neither mysterious nor complex as a concept, and I have deliberately used the term '**working** relationship'. The intention is not to know and understand each other's deepest emotions, make friends, or invest in spending time together for pleasure, although all of these things may sometimes happen, but to achieve sufficient understanding and trust to work together. The individual needs to understand the social worker's role, and the purpose of the assessment.

The social worker needs to get down to the business of working out the individual's future plans. This is as good a way of establishing a productive working relationship as any. This does not preclude being friendly, but does mean avoiding the kind of activity that sometimes passes for social work: all 'social' and no 'work'.

Timing is crucial to assessment. Getting both the time of the assessment and the length of time taken right is vital. In relation to hospital discharge, for example, assessing people too early will over emphasise dependency (assuming they are in the process of getting better). Whether they are at home or in hospital, it is always necessary to ascertain whether someone is fit enough to participate in the assessment process. Even the time of day may be important for some people, and produce far different outcomes. The length of time also matters: most social workers feel constrained to do assessments too fast these days, especially as they know that many people have difficulties in communication of one kind or another. However, for other people, the assessment process is only a hurdle before opportunities for improvement, and there is no point for them in taking too long over it.

Before embarking on any assessment, the social worker needs to have sorted out what the assessment is all about and ensure that her purpose and aims in undertaking it are in agreement with those of the individual concerned. It will either be related to a particular issue or problem presented by the individual themselves, or highlighted by a third party, or a more general assessment initiated under some piece of legislation, such as for school leaving.

The first stage is to ensure that the individual shares an understanding with the worker about:

THE GROUNDRULES

i   the purpose of the assessment

ii   how it will be undertaken

iii   how long it will take

iv   who will have an input into it

v   the need for interpreters or advocates

vi   how it will be recorded

vii   who will see the results

viii   what will happen to any documentation

ix   what the possible outcomes are

x   what the limits to the assessment are

xi   any rights of appeal

This shared understanding is a necessary underpinning without which there is an increased risk of breaches of trust when the process does not meet the individual's expectations. As such, establishing the ground rules in this way is part and parcel of the process of building a trusting relationship. It establishes the worker as a professional helper, and not simply a friend. Social workers have a job to do, and people expect them to get down to the business of doing it. Having said that, it is acknowledged that establishing trust with a child may take more than a reasonable explanation of what the assessment is all about, but it does not excuse us from undertaking that explanation – as far as is possible, given the age and understanding of the child.

It is important to tell the truth, even when it is unwelcome, and not to make promises that cannot be kept. Skating over unpleasant facts may bring short term progress but is ultimately unhelpful. Promises to keep in touch and to revisit are commonly broken. This destroys confidence not only in the worker in question, but in all of her colleagues. It is vital not to promise confidentiality where there is a responsibility to share information. If assessment documentation is to form the basis of reports to an assessment panel, the individual has a right to know who is on that panel, and the use that will be made of the information provided. The worker should make it clear she will not knowingly give a misleading impression of the individual's circumstances, and may wish to record things that she can observe to be true as well as things that the individual reports. The most obvious issues concern abuse, but there is a range of other issues affecting sick or disabled people and their carers where individual stress or ill health is creating observable difficulties on which carer and cared for may not agree. It is well known that social workers need to use their eyes, and noses come to that. They should check their observations with people, and not secretly record them. To do so is dishonest, but it may also be inaccurate. An observed difficulty may be a very temporary problem or something more lasting, and only asking is likely to distinguish which it is. It is also a way of introducing subjects which should be aired, but about which the individual is embarrassed, or which they do not consider relevant: 'I notice you are limping, Mrs. Green. Is that usual?'

ACKNOWLEDGING EMOTION

Part of establishing a working relationship is to acknowledge and release any negative feelings which may be evident, and deal with them if possible. Assessments happen all too often when people are at their most vulnerable, and when they may be feeling at their least competent. They may be recovering from illness; in pain; grieving for someone; or facing the loss of their home. In many cases, it may be the first time in their lives that they have been in the position of having to seek help with personal care, or with the care of those close to them. There are issues about loss of control and independence that may be damaging to self image. The individual may feel angry, let down, humiliated, frightened, depressed, distressed or stigmatised. She may feel resistant to having to ask for help or to discussing private concerns with strangers, or she may be embarrassed at showing her feelings or revealing her vulnerability.

The social worker can help not only by acknowledging and legitimating these feelings, but also by making a conscious effort to ensure that the assessment process does not add to them. Indeed, if conducted properly, it should add to self esteem. One important fact to emphasise is that the assessment is focusing on the person's situation, and is related to her perceptions and aspirations. While it may include judgements about her personal capabilities and personality, it is not an MOT test. There are no pass or fail standards against which people are measured. Collecting only relevant data, which is related to the actual situation will help retain confidence, as will ensuring that the individual has the opportunity to examine any recorded information before it goes elsewhere. This helps to establish an honest basis for dealing based on mutual respect rather than the social worker abdicating responsibility for it or feeling obliged to exclude relevant data because it is unpalatable.

STAGE TWO: DATA COLLECTION
ASPIRATIONS — WHAT THE INDIVIDUAL WANTS

The next stage is to find out what the individual wants, either as an immediate result of the assessment or more broadly during the foreseeable future. Making a conscious effort to start where the individual is at reduces the risk of imposing standards or ideas on them. They may not want things for themselves that most people want, or that the social worker thinks they should want. There is a growing concern in social work not to make assumptions based on differences such as race, gender, sexuality, or age. It is also worth being aware that it is perhaps those individuals who are most like us, or who are in situations which parallel our own experience – who are at the greatest risk of our making assumptions about how they are feeling and reacting, and about what they want from life.

This may mean unstitching preconceived, and limited ideas about services available. Individuals do not arrive at the assessment process with untainted minds, but will have all kinds of notions about what they can expect, or not expect, and what they have to do to get a particular service. Some of the process of wiping the slate clean will have occurred if the first stage is effectively completed. The chances are, however, that individuals will have expectations and ideas for the future based on someone else's experience or the advice of, say, a consultant or next door's home help. These may be unrealistically high or, more likely, low. In my experience, potential service users have low expectations, and even if asked for their ideal outcome rarely come up with anything outrageous. The kind of people who are most likely to experience assessment are those whom life has taught to expect little, and to have to fight hard even for that. It is therefore good practice to be fairly persistent in establishing this basic information, and checking its continuing validity as the assessment proceeds.

BARRIERS

Barriers are at various levels from personal and family, to institutional and societal. For the purposes of assessment it is helpful to think of them as two main groups: barriers to achieving ambitions or goals, and barriers to accepting help. The second is discussed where it might more logically fall in the assessment process... after 'Sources of support'.

Personal barriers to achievement or independent living mean an individual or family not having sufficient faith in themselves to have a go, or to take a risk. Failure to reach goals in life is disappointing, but it is part and parcel of it, and no reason not to try. Yet there is a Catch 22 operating here. Confident people who do not fear failure, will laugh about it, dust themselves off and try again. They are actually more likely to succeed than those who are less confident, fear ridicule or who carry the hopes and dreams of others with them. It is harder, for example, for a black woman to become Lord High Anything because she is watched and judged at every step in a way that a white man does not have to endure. Members of oppressed groups have to be better than average in order to succeed, have to follow the rules to the letter, and have to be prepared to take every step in the glare of publicity, or at least the judgemental appraisal of others. They are not allowed to be mediocre.

People internalise oppression, and carry deep-seated beliefs that they are not as good as others, and do not deserve success or even opportunity. These are hard to unpick, as they are often masked by aggression or a host of well-rehearsed reasons for not trying to do something. This can even result in people jeopardising their own plans or destroying their own work to avoid the risk of failure.

People with low self esteem may not believe in their own ability or right to success because of an internalised belief that able-bodied people, or heterosexuals, or white people are somehow intrinsically more deserving and **better** than they are. They require careful and patient support, preferably from a peer group. If not, failure becomes a self-fulfilling prophecy.

Institutional barriers to achieving ambitions and goals are also going to be problematic, although highlighting them is usually less contentious, since talking about them does not negatively impact on someone's personality or self esteem. It is naive to suppose that society is anything other than oppressive, and that it does not create more difficulties for some of its members than others. In identifying barriers that prevent individuals achieving goals, it is worth remembering that many of them affect many people who share certain characteristics. Tackling them therefore may best be undertaken on a collective basis. Disabled children are disadvantaged by discriminatory abortion laws, inequitable health care, segregated education and the failure of childcare services to offer protection from abuse, as well as by the more obvious problems of prejudice among employers and lack of physical access to buildings.

Black people are disadvantaged by racist attacks, poor health care, high unemployment and a range of pathologising prejudices about their behaviour. Much of health and welfare is perceived as run by white people for white people. There are a range of myths about black people which are used as justifications for inadequate or non existent services: *"they look after their own"* is a classic example, as is the frequent 'there are no black people in this area'.

Gay people who want to foster children, train as social workers, care for their partners or to be protected from institutional abuse face a raft of prejudice, ignorance and hostility.

Institutional barriers translate at local level into the hostile neighbour, the clique at the play group or the bully at work, all of whom are given informal permission to exclude, ridicule or harass by the wider prejudices of society. These attitudes create a great deal of misery for isolated families and individuals, and need to be tackled on a local basis. It is sometimes just ignorance and fear.

STRESSES AND CONCERNS

The next pieces of data collection concern two sides of the same coin. The assessment will need to include information both on sources of stress/problems/ concerns/fears on the one hand, and to collect information on resources and coping mechanisms, or the individual's usual way of dealing with difficulties, on the other.

There are myriads of causes of stress for people, and

those in the box are just some examples. Some things worry some people more than others, and it does not help to impose the social worker's own worries on someone whose concerns may be quite different.

Something quite minor may have assumed a position of overwhelming importance in someone's worry stakes: the old saying about the camel's back is worth remembering. It is also true that when the big things in life seem unresolvable and impossible, it is the little things we rant and rave about!

> **DATA COLLECTION: SOURCES OF STRESS**
> - Finances
> - Housing
> - Lack of transport
> - Family, or other relationship problems
> - Neighbourhood or community pressure
> - Problems at work/school
> - Ill health
> - Bullying
> - Unemployment
> - Too much responsibility
> - Loss
> - Lack of sleep
> - Abuse
> - Racism/racist attacks
> - Harassment
> - Poor service provision
> - Fear of abusive carers

RESOURCES/SOURCES OF SUPPORT

Only after establishing what the individual wants, is it appropriate to undertake a review of resources. Some social workers prefer to undertake this exercise before embarking on the problems and barriers, and while there are sound reasons for this in terms of building up a positive picture, in practice most individuals want any problems aired early on. It is still helpful to spend some time talking about personal, family and community resources in a fairly systematic way, as there are often more positives than people realise, and it can be empowering for the individual to be the source of such positive information. The social worker and the individual should combine their knowledge to list all the sources of support, used and unused, that are available, or that might be made available.

Resources can be internal and external to the individual and should include both practical and personal resources.

The box gives some examples of the kind of resources which might be included in such a review. Needless to say, while the individual is the worker's best source of information on most of these, a worker who knows her patch should be able to add to the Practical List, if only by collecting information from one individual and passing it on.

This exercise will identify resource gaps, both practical and personal, as well as gaps in knowledge which either the social worker or the individual should take responsibility for filling.

DATA COLLECTION: RESOURCES

Practical
- Financial resources
- Housing type, size, accessibility
- Baby-sitting circles
- Shops
- Home deliveries
- Voluntary organisations
- Playgroups
- Family
- Neighbours
- Church/mosque or similar
- Peer, support or pressure groups

Personal
- Health
- Spiritual beliefs
- Self-help techniques
- Sense of humour
- Education
- Strength of character
- Outlook on life
- Skills
- Physical strength
- Mental strength

COPING MECHANISMS

These should be discussed and drawn out as part of the assessment process, but it is worth remembering that the assessment itself can be part of a healing process. Just as it is important at the start to acknowledge and legitimate feelings which individuals have about entering into an assessment process, it is also necessary to recognise that the process itself may give rise to emotion. Emotional difficulties which emerge during the assessment process will inevitably have to be dealt with by the worker.

While the worker should remain clear in her mind which activity she is involved in at any one time, and may have to be clear with the individual about the limits to any therapeutic help she can offer personally, identifying emotional stress is going to be an integral part of assessment in many cases. Releasing such feelings can start the healing process, as well as assist the individual and the worker identify an appropriate way forward which acknowledges and legitimates the grief or the anger. Sharing feelings, whether by crying, shouting or hugging, with a professional worker in confidence is often a helpful step. No reciprocation is required and there should be no embarrassing aftermath. Nor is it necessary for the purpose of the assessment to record anything about the behaviour, as opposed to the reasons behind it.

In parallel with establishing what creates stress, or difficulty for any individual in particular, her methods and means of coping should also be established. This means that recommendations for the future can build on existing strengths and preferred ways of working, rather than inventing something new or suggesting something inappropriate. The worker should shed any preconceptions before starting this exercise. All young people do not necessarily unwind to loud rock music, nor are all

> **DATA COLLECTION: COPING MECHANISMS**
> - Planning ahead
> - Meditation
> - Drink
> - Solitude
> - Religion
> - Talking things over
> - One day at a time philosophy
> - Television
> - Long soapy bath
> - Company of friends
> - Support group
> - Dear Diary
> - Work
> - Sport/Leisure
> - Fighting the system
> - 'Kicking the Cat'
> - Hiding in a shell
> - Music: playing/listening

old women lovers of Jesus. The list in the Coping Mechanisms box is therefore to be treated with care! Many of the coping mechanisms are directly opposed to each other, while others can go very nicely together. Some, clearly, can become problems in themselves if overdone. Drinking too much is obvious, but other activities such as work as an escape from difficulties at home are perhaps less easy to identify. 'Kicking the Cat' is a generic term for passing on anger and frustration, which can be therapeutic if the target is inanimate, but not if a child becomes the punchbag. Some coping mechanisms that help one individual in a group may work to the exclusion, financial ruin, or detriment of others. The social worker should be aiming to identify helpful coping mechanisms within a individual, which can be built on, strengthened, or supported. Discussion around these areas can be helpful in itself, and enables individuals to discover their own powers and their own ways of healing.

BARRIERS TO ACCEPTING HELP

On a practical level this includes things like resources being too far away from home, at inconvenient times, too expensive, too posh, too poor, too white or black/Asian or physically inaccessible.

On a psychological level, there are all kinds of reasons why people find it hard to accept help, which may require sensitive counselling. These range from embarrassment and shyness, fear of the unfamiliar and not knowing what to do, to deep-seated feelings of guilt and lack of self worth.

Parents may be embarrassed by an incontinent, badly behaved, or unusual child and find it easier to stay at home than to keep explaining.

Fear of criticism about childcare or nursing standards may run high with many individuals, even within the extended family group. Children and adults often behave better for temporary carers than they do for those close to them.

Receiving help at home means allowing strangers to see, and perhaps judge, standards of housekeeping, eating or sleeping habits. Some families may be using their homes for criminal or political activity. This may be serious such as fencing stolen property, prostitution, or making pornographic videos, but it may be activities which are less socially damaging such as having an undeclared lodger, keeping a banned pet in a council flat, or operating a small business.

Their activities may or may not be illegal, but families may nevertheless not wish anyone official to know. The social services will be quite uninterested in many such activities, but what matters is how the family believes that social services, or other helpers in their home, will react.

A common barrier to accepting help is the inability to reciprocate. Many people dislike taking something for nothing, and the impracticability of returning favours can deter, even if for some offering help is reward in itself and no return favour is required. In such cases, people may find that state help, or help they pay for, is easier to accept.

A more serious concern for individuals and carers is the fear of abuse from temporary carers, either at home, in day care, or more especially in residential institutions. This ranges from the belief that residential staff will not care as well as the full-time carer can, to much more serious fears of physical and sexual abuse. There is sufficient evidence of both of these scenarios to make these fears realistic, and to be taken seriously. Social workers can and should take practical steps to minimise such risks, either by supporting the individual's own efforts, or those of a group of service users, or by building safeguards into service contracts. Simple requirements such as there always being two adults on a bus with a group of children can go a long way to reassure those who fear that perpetrators of abuse may seek unsupervised work with children.

In addition there are concerns about self image associated with accepting help, welfare or charity, such as not wanting to be identified as a problem family, or as someone who cannot cope. The consistent use of the language of rights can be helpful, by transferring the sense of responsibility from the individual or family to that of the wider society. Few people have trouble accepting medical assistance, or hesitate to call out the fire brigade, because such services are seen as part and parcel of life in a society into which contributions are made and from which resources are drawn.

EXPERT EVIDENCE

It may be appropriate in some assessments to seek advice or information concerning the individual from experts, such as occupational therapists, educationalists, psychologists or from medical practitioners. Once obtained, it cannot be set aside if someone disagrees, although second opinions may be sought by either the social worker or the individual. The use to be made of any such information should be made clear to the individual concerned, and it is also important to be clear to the person providing it that it will be made available to the subject. This requires careful handling. Medical information, in particular, may be seen by the individual for the first time during the assessment. The social worker should be prepared to ask the medical practitioner to give the patient time to discuss anything she does not understand about it. This is always preferable to the social worker acting as interpreter. On the other hand, some medical personnel will only provide information on the basis that the individual does not see it, resulting in odd bits in files which are 'confidential'. Access to health records can still be denied to patients if the record holder believes it would cause them or others harm to disclose it.

This can result in unreasonable withholding of information. While no one should be forced to read their medical files, it is authoritarian to deny access to adults who request it. Nevertheless, it may be the only way to secure information that helps obtain services which are desirable. Patients denied such access should ask to see the organisation's policy statement on disclosure, and be prepared to challenge it if their particular doctor seems un-cooperative.

STAGE THREE: ANALYSIS

The analysis of data is the key to a good assessment. The quality of data collected is clearly important, but it is what is made of it that really counts. It is no use expecting answers to emerge like magic from the data. Information should have been collected in terms of its relevance to the aspirations of the individual, and in relation to any problems she presented or changes she wishes to make. The analysis should have similar relevance, and is the search for options to enable decisions to be made.

If data proves insufficient or inadequate, then more information will have to be sought, but there is no point in collecting more and more data simply for the sake of it. It is a matter of being clear from the outset what questions are being asked, and what you need to know to answer them.

It is worth re-stating what the individual wants at this point. The purpose of the assessment may have shifted during the process: if so, this should be clearly acknowledged and agreed. The next step will be to identify the changes in the individual's situation which are required to achieve the desired ends, identifying any risks and how they might be managed. List opportunities for achieving change, including service options. Note and agree any role for possible service providers, and then consider which service provider, assuming it is not obvious. The pros and cons of each possible way forward need to be weighed, and this includes costing. It is often useful to draw these up as a chart, and many organisations have useful pro forma for this kind of activity. If not, any large piece of blank paper will serve. It is important to note that this is part of the decision making process, and not the final plan. It is therefore quite legitimate, indeed desirable, to include options and ideas which may seem hard to put into place, or about which there is limited information. They can always be scrubbed out later.

Making assessment a positive experience for the individual means involving them fully during this process, including the flip charts and pens, or the biro on the back of an envelope. It means sharing with them gaps in knowledge that either the worker or the individual might go back and fill in later; it means letting the individual include possibilities even if a feasibility discussion knocks them out of the picture for one reason or another. The social worker's preferred option, even if the individual is not keen, also has a legitimate place at this stage, with the same understanding about its possible lack of a long term future.

When it is over, the analysis should have identified the aspirations or nature of the problem, or risk, what changes are necessary, and what service options are preferred. In assessing the value of any service option, the question of its usefulness in achieving or working toward the desired changes should be answered. This may seem obvious, but discussions do have a mysterious habit of drifting away from the point!

The next stage is about putting the decision into practice by arranging the care package. It involves exploration about feasibility, the negotiation of terms, and the provision for review. There is no point in setting objectives which those responsible for executing cannot envisage putting into practice. It is at this stage that the assessment process overlaps with the care planning... the baton is prepared for passing over. Timing is crucial, as is the fact that the assessor only has a certain amount of time before she has to hand over.

STAGE FOUR. PLANNING

DRAFT PROPOSALS AND NEGOTIATION

Draft proposals will result from the analysis and will then be subject to negotiation with possible service providers, with the individual and with whoever holds the purse. All three parties matter if the outcome is to be a feasible and acceptable plan. (There may of course, be more than three parties.)

The social worker engaged in this process is undertaking not only a balancing act in relation to this particular case, but also in relation to others both current and in the future. It is little use in the long term driving a smart bargain with a service provider, or even not telling them the whole truth, since both tactics may result in closed options in the future. The same dilemmas will affect independent advocates, unless they plan to move around the country at high speed and leave their histories behind them. This means trying to reach an arrangement which is mutually beneficial – a win/win situation, if you like – rather than settling for poor service, or not trying to secure the best possible deal.

Earlier sections of this text have indicated that this is not always going to be easy, and that there are both overt and covert agendas to take into account. The more open the process the better. If the individual does have to settle for second best, she should at least be clear why, and able to see that the social worker has made the effort. I always preferred to have clients in the room with me when ringing the DSS or Housing departments on their behalf. Although it hampered my ability to collude, it saved time later convincing the individual that the call had been duly made – and that every effort had been made on their behalf.

Negotiations proceed with all parties on a 'what if... will you?' basis, until agreement is reached. They may involve a number of agencies in a complex package, so recording all provisional agreements is vital. It is usually counter-productive to force people into accepting the kind of help they do not really want. Their willingness to use it and ability to benefit will be limited.

Nor should the welfare of the child or dependent adult be subjugated to the needs of the parent or carer because it is convenient, pragmatic or speedier to do so rather than search for a way forward which benefits both.

RECOMMENDATIONS

Recommendations should follow from the analysis of the data and the outcome of negotiations. This may seem obvious, but as a service manager on the receiving end of assessments, I became very used to reading through documents only to reach a concluding section which began optimistically with... 'therefore...', but which bore no relation whatsoever to anything that had gone before!

Recommendations should relate to the negotiations around provision, and it follows that there may be some feedback process around these two tasks, in order that the final recommendations are feasible and acceptable to the individual and to the service providers.

It makes no sense to set a target that is unattainable. In many cases this does not mean abandoning goals but prioritising objectives to render them feasible. Much can be achieved in a planned sequence that seems quite impossible to handle at one go.

ARRANGEMENTS FOR REVIEW

No assessment lasts for ever. It is simply the process by which decisions are made and should not be added to the casefile as a life plan or definitive document. It is an evolving and ongoing process, and whatever plan is put into place as a result will require review. This may be informal and unrecorded if it involves no service provision, but if it does then it is vital to ensure that arrangements are made for review. This does not necessarily mean reassessment, nor that the social worker returns like an avenging angel. The review arrangements are as individual as the initial assessment, and should be built into it.

Key questions for review arrangements
- how will we know if our plans are working?
- if they are not, is it the plan that needs revision, or the way it is being put into practice?
- who will take responsibility for this review?
- when will it take place?
- what arrangements should we make to review early, if necessary?

If services are used, directly or indirectly, then these will be subject to contract, either with the consumer directly or through the social services. Getting the specifications right is part of the assessment process, and the point at which purchaser hands over to provider. The issue of how these will be measured, and when, has to be included from the outset. This may mean the individual reporting back to the social worker; it may mean a pre-arranged review meeting to talk over the original aims and whether the service is still appropriate. It may mean the service provider being asked to produce a written report at regular intervals. In any case, the review has to relate to the original assessment, and to be tested against the plans which came out of it.

It is appreciated that social workers are not going to have time to review directly all those receiving services paid for by social services. The sheer volume of assessments will preclude this, but there is nothing new in people being 'placed' by local authorities and then quietly forgotten about except by the computer in the finance department. To be realistic, review quality will vary, but it should be possible to devise systems whereby those whose situations are most volatile or give rise for concern are given priority for direct review or re-assessment, while the rest are dealt with indirectly.

This latter means reaching agreement with service providers about giving key information to the purchaser on a regular basis so that service quality can be estimated, and problems highlighted. A random sample of direct visits – to the individual's home or to residential or day care provision – to supplement this should weed out any service providers tempted to fabricate! Purchasers need to identify the kind of information necessary for indirect review, to be agreed as part of the service agreement with providers internal and external. This may include the provider conducting a review with the service user, and sending a written report to the purchaser. Basic indicators such as the presence or absence of the service user, his or her family, friends or advocates, place and length of time of discussion and issues raised will begin to give a picture of the quality of the process. This is not as arduous as it may first appear. For many service users the basic service specifications will be similar, as will be the process for review. Adding individual touches in each case should not prove unduly difficult.

The recorded arrangements for review will identify the responsible people and the timing and nature of the review. '**Who** will do **what** by **when**?' are useful things to clarify before leaving the negotiating table!

MEASURING A QUALITY ASSESSMENT

One measure of a good assessment will be the quality of the service which arises from it. Service users are becoming increasingly critical of inflexible and inappropriate services. One powerful advocate for improvement is Jenny Morris, and her book *Independent Lives* published in 1993 raises a number of questions about the quality of service delivery. These informed the questions raised on p66 which identifies some aspects of good and bad service delivery.

The challenge is to approach assessments in such a way that the answers to the kind of questions posed are positive, produce outcomes which preserve the dignity of the service user, and do not add to their oppression. Clearly, given the range of influences on the outcome, this is not always easy, and is certainly not wholly within the control of an individual undertaking an assessment. Nevertheless, professionals owe it to people in need of help to approach the business of assessment with the intention of producing results which are reasonable and which are equitable. The tables on p67, reproduced from an article in *Care Weekly* (1994), are some of the characteristics of good and bad assessment.

SOCIAL SERVICES

ASPECTS OF GOOD AND BAD PRACTICE

Do services fit people's lives or the other way around?

Does a person have a choice of when she gets put to bed, has her meal?

Do home helps do housework?

ARE SERVICES RESPONSIVE?

Will meals on wheels deliver to workplaces?

Are services flexible, increasing when people are unwell, for example, or if the weather is bad?

DO SERVICES RESTRICT PEOPLE?

Will home helps only help inside the home?

Will Crossroads only help if the carer goes out?

DO YOU HAVE TO FIT A PERSON TO A SERVICE?

Are people forced to medicalise their need? Claim problems they do not have? Emphasising disability can be a passport to financial and practical help.

WILL YOU GET A BETTER SERVICE IF YOU ARE AN AMENABLE PERSON, PREPARED TO COMPROMISE?

Demanding people aren't liked. Do people who are grateful and do not argue get a better deal?

RELATIONSHIPS WITH OFFICIAL CARERS

Does the helper expect gratitude/obedience? Is she insulting, patronising, controlling, judgmental, abusive, homophobic? You can't chose your care assistant, and she might be the sort of person you wouldn't normally invite home.

PRIVACY

Do carers respect privacy, or treat people's homes as an extension of an institution... giving them rights to use things, answer the door, use the phone, arrange things?

Is information passed on, for example about someone's sexuality?

ASSUMPTIONS THAT FAMILY WILL CARE

Do service providers make untested assumptions about the willingness of people to care for relatives, or that the disabled or sick person wants help from their relatives?

GOOD ASSESSMENT

Starts with an open mind

Starts where the individual is

Involves and empowers the user as a partner

Relates to their perceived problem and explores the reasons for it

Collects only relevant data

Puts the information in the context of its collection

Analyses the problem using the data

Explores the pros and cons of a range of solutions

Thinks about a range of options

Does not put pressure on the user to choose the option the assessor wants

Negotiates with the individual, and with existing and potential service providers, to find an acceptable and feasible solution

Makes recommendations which relate to the information collected

Makes arrangements for review

BAD ASSESSMENT

Diminishes the user

Leaves too much power in the hands of the assessor

Starts with a preconceived idea of what the solution is, or what service may be required

Does not differentiate between individuals but puts them all through the same process

Does not trouble to discuss individual concerns

Does not involve the user, and may even rely on a third party or observed data only

Relies on a tick box form as a crutch for unskilled workers

Uses an MOT type approach to the person, against an established view of what is normal

Lays the difficulties at the door of the person, rather than having some appreciation of their circumstances

Talks of individual strengths and weaknesses, not aspirations, frustrations, lack of resources or disabling environments

Collects data for the sake of it, relating it neither to the perceived problem, nor the recommended care package

Does not explore options

Uses no imagination

Takes services from a shelf of ready-made goods, rather than creates a custom-built individual response

Assumes the assessment has a long shelf-life and does not relate it to the time, place and circumstances of its being undertaken

Reprinted from 'Care Weekly' Jan 20 1994

Professional and management issues

**While social work professionals can provide the value
base, skills and experience to undertake high quality
assessments, these cannot work without a measure of
organisational support and the commitment of
management to a good service. Much of this involves
accepting the rights of people to information, respect
and as much choice as imagination and resources
permit. It also means acknowledging that good
assessment does take time, and can be stressful. What
appears to be more stressful than the encounters with
service users are the conflicts which workers report
within their own organisations and which relate to the
perceived value put on their work.**

Typically, social services departments are increasingly
undertaking assessments with fewer workers and with a
lower value placed on their professional qualifications.

Major decisions have to be made about who is
conducting assessments and who is receiving them. There
are temptations for resource-strapped organisations to
reduce the numbers of assessments, not only because they
cost money to conduct but because they create demands
for services once completed. This reduction can be
achieved either by cutting numbers of assessment staff or
by restricting eligibility criteria so that fewer people get
through the gateway into the process.

Having fewer people doing assessments means each
person doing more and working faster. This involves
finding mechanisms for speeding the process so that it
becomes mechanistic and formula based.

Social workers faced with the mindlessness of
completing pages and pages of tick boxes can feel
deskilled and devalued by the process. Social work
involves listening, reflecting, supporting, nudging and
negotiating. the pressure to complete x number of forms
of whatever quality by lunch time is demoralising.

The latter approach, of raising the threshold for eligibility for assessment and restricting service provision only to the highly dependent, encourages people to exaggerate or reframe their problems in order to access services. Typically, this means the medicalisation of difficulties, but it can mean threats of harm to dependants or children, or threats of suicide, all of which may become real. The failure of health and social services to provide basic levels of support services in the community is coupled with a crisis-only response.

The end result of either scenario is an increase in poor work, ill-considered assessments and resultant poor service, and human misery. This dismal picture is not helped by continuing territorial disputes between health and social services in some areas. Acknowledgement by each that both are strapped for cash would be a constructive starting point from which to allocate resources and responsibilities. It is a pity that some managers appear to prefer the expensive pastime of sniping at each other.

In an age of litigation, the better informed will undoubtedly take up even more valuable professional time by instituting complaints and reviews.

Assessments are legal processes, and therefore subject to official scrutiny. Local authorities must have complaints procedures in place. Maladministration is subject to review by the Commissioner for Local Administration (Ombudsman). Failure to stick to due process in decision making is subject to judicial review through the courts and local authorities will be penalised if they do not reach appropriate standards. Managers need to ensure that individuals legally entitled to assessment are not denied one, and that the waiting time is reasonable. They will need to demonstrate that all relevant facts have been considered. Restrictive practices increasingly will be challenged as solicitors learn their way around these procedures.

There is therefore a choice for management between encouraging the kind of high quality assessment which has been described in this text, or accepting bad practice and shortcuts with the risk of having to justify them:

the courts. It is accepted that given the severe constraints in local government, this is not an easy choice, and some authorities taking an actuarial perspective may conclude that the risk of costly litigation is minimal compared with the cost of high quality practice. Small wonder, in such organisations, that there is a squeeze on professionals whose code of ethics would find such calculations quite unacceptable.

CONCLUSION: TOWARD ANTI-OPPRESSIVE PRACTICE

So where does all this leave us? I have been advocating assessment as a value-based activity that involves exploring a person's situation, looking for ways to improve it and identifying services which help toward that end. While it is concerned with effecting change for an individual or group, an assessment is about someone within a specific context. Both the elements of the person and the situation are important, and it is pointless to assess one without the other. In working out options for change, either the person or the situation can be the focus.

I have tried to point out the various pressures which work against assessment working smoothly and efficiently. Effective assessors need to learn to operate and negotiate within an understanding of these conflicting pressures, rather than simply keep complaining that expectations are unfair or that their jobs are impossible.

This is the real world. It is not equitable, nor, crucially, do a great many powerful people wish it to be so. In practice, the options will often be very limited, and ways forward hard to see at all. Changing much of this will only be effected by working collectively through political or professional organisations. In many cases, assessment will be more about damage limitation than real improvement for people who find themselves in no-win situations or facing serious losses. At the very least the social worker can strive to ensure that the assessment itself is experienced as positive and that the individual gains from the process of working out their own future prospects.

Respect for individual difference is an essential value basis for undertaking assessment if the individual is to feel enhanced rather than diminished by the experience.

Beyond that simple tolerance, a good social worker will need to develop and learn ways of challenging oppression, not only in the mean streets of society, but also that oppression which is internalised within the individuals themselves. Oppression is not simply how the more powerful think of us, and how they act on that, it is about how we are made to think and feel about ourselves, and how we act on that. It is this self-perception as being second class which prevents people from achieving their potential as much as any overt and obvious discriminatory practices, and it is infinitely harder to deal with.

Some individuals will have a lifetime of experience of being shunned and segregated, and will approach assessment by social services with resignation, cynicism, defiance... or joy depending on how they have personally dealt with the issues and their own previous experience of welfare or health services.

Society expects its members to fit in, and operates powerful sanctions to encourage conformity. It follows that those who deviate must either be deliberately wicked or sick, and as such cannot expect to be treated as full citizens or deserve to receive equality of opportunity.

There are strong pressures to avoid being negatively labelled, even though many of the factors which exclude are characteristics quite outside individual control such as race, sexual orientation and disability. The aspect most likely to alter in any life is that of disability, and those who become disabled not only face the implications of the impairment itself, but also face the prospects of joining the ranks of those who are discriminated against, and therefore perhaps of meeting their own beliefs about the meaning of disability from the other side. The reaction will be very individual, and complex.

For some the experience of loss of control produced by needing help from health or social services may be something quite new. Efforts to conform to a meaning of normality and to retain a positive self-image may involve such things as rejecting the use of wheelchairs or sticks, even though they would improve mobility, since both are powerful symbols of dependency.

On the other hand, those whose beliefs support a social

model of disability, in which the problems encountered by disabled people are attributed to discrimination by society, may have difficulty in accepting the legitimacy of their personal experience of frustration, despair or depression at the very real pain, incapacity or tiredness caused by an impairment. These feelings are complicated even more when the incapacity is someone else's, such as that of a child. These are difficult areas in which to work, where even acknowledging the quandaries can sometimes unwittingly cause offence.

Clearly, there is a great deal more to a good assessment than adding up needs, and matching them to services

Social workers undertaking assessments will not unravel all this, but they can play a part. Emphasising people's rights to consultation, control and choice during assessment will retain or help to restore self respect. Workers undertaking assessment as a matter of routine should not forget what it may mean as a unique experience for the individual concerned.

It follows that individuals cannot always be deemed to be "experts on their own needs or situations", despite the simplistic rhetoric that has mushroomed around such slogans. Indeed such ideas not only represent an avoidance of responsibility by professional helpers, but can be deeply disempowering for people who find themselves in new situations and need help. The sudden onset of disability is one situation few people consider before it happens to them, partly because most people's knowledge of disability is informed by media and charity images of helplessness and tragedy. Parents are not always the best people to represent the needs of their disabled children: not because they do not care, but because the experience of what disability means is largely limited to those who have direct experience of it. Parents of a disabled child may have no means of knowing what to ask for, which can result in the child receiving minimum services. **(Sloper and Turner 1992)** There is a clear professional role in widening horizons, taking a longer term perspective, ensuring the interests of the child remain central to the process, and working out ways to help both child and parents understand and counter the disablism they are bound to face. (**Middleton 1996**)

Helping without diminishing people's dignity and self-respect is a skilled activity. It takes social work as a professional activity a long way from medical models of helping which are based on expert diagnosis and prescription. Much of what is prescribed is devised by drug companies and fails to tackle or even acknowledge the underlying issues, leaving its users dependent and pathologised. Social work means helping people identify what their choices are – based not only on the person's own awareness and knowledge, but also utilising the experiences of other people with whom the social worker has interacted before. Part of the social workers stock in trade is to make use of past experience of what helps and what hurts to aid them in helping and facilitating others. It follows that social work education, at whatever level, should be concerned with enabling practitioners to reflect critically on their experience in order to make informed use of it.

It is the quality of the dynamic between the social worker and the person being assessed that will distinguish a good assessment from a bad one. This means both the worker and the individual concerned being prepared to listen, to explore possibilities, to understand risk and to respect and trust each other.

Self-confidence and self-respect can be maintained or built by involving people in their own life choices, even when these are hard choices: indeed, perhaps, **especially** when they are hard choices. After all it is more important to choose where to live or where to die than the colour of the wallpaper, although ironically some people will undoubtedly spend more time in deliberating about the latter or be given more time to do so.

It may be the social worker rather than the service user who has difficulties with their self-confidence. This book has described many of the organisational pressures that militate against good practice and hinder workers from doing a good job. The greater such pressures, the more likely it is that assessments will be skimped, done badly, and not be a source of pride for those involved. Social workers who care about quality are in danger of becoming disenchanted. It is incumbent on everyone concerned with the quality of health and welfare services to continue to point out that poorly-trained and ill-educated professionals represent incalculable human misery to those on the receiving end of poor service.

Professional social work, under whatever guise it comes to operate in the future, is about effecting change in people's lives. It needs to retain its commitment to working in a collaborative manner, toward civil rights for all adults and children, and to avoid becoming the unthinking tool of bureaucracy. This means reaffirming the basic values that underpin professional practice, and believing in the possibility of effecting change.

Assessment, formal or informal, is central in that it is the process by which decisions are reached about attaining, maintaining or retaining a desirable lifestyle. It matters that it is done well, not only for the individuals concerned but as the key to appropriate and sound welfare services. It also matters that it is understood to be only a part of the work of effecting change, and that services, support and review follow from it.

While much of what is recommended as good practice in this book may seem idealistic to people struggling to maintain services in the face of pressures to make cuts, it is essential that we retain a vision of how it ought to be. Only with a destination in mind, have we any hope of knowing whether or not we are on the right road.

References

Bradshaw, Jonathan. (1972) 'The concept of human need' *New Society* March 30th

Coulshed, Veronica (1988) *Social Work Practice* Macmillan

Common R and Flynn, N (1992) *Contracting for Care* Community Care/Rowntree Trust

Eley R and Middleton L(1983) 'Square Pegs, round holes? The appropriateness of providing care for old people in residential settings' *Health Trends* Vol 15, 3. 68-70

Department of Health (1995) *Building Bridges: A guide to arrangements for inter agency working for the care and protection of severely mentally ill people* HMSO

Department of Health/Social Services Inspectorate (1991) *Care Management and Assessment: Manager's Guide* HMSO

Department of Health/Social Services Inspectorate (1991) *Care Management and Assessment: Practitioners' Guide* HMSO

Department of Health (1991) *The Children Act 1989 Guidance and Regulations* (9 vols) HMSO

Halford, Alison (1993) *No way up the greasy pole* Constable

Middleton, Laura (1994) 'Little Boxes are not enough' *Care Weekly* Number 306 January 20

Middleton L (1996) *Making a Difference: Social work with disabled children* Birmingham, Venture Press

Morris, Jenny (1993) *Independent Lives: Community Care and Disabled People* London, Macmillan

Platt, Denise (1990) 'Assessment and Case Management: Practical Implications of Implemnting the Draft Circular' in Isobel Allen (ed) *Assessment And Case Management* Department of Heath/Policy Studies Institute/Association of Directors of Social Services

Social Services Inspectorate (1991) *Getting the Message Across* HMSO

Sloper P and Turner S (1992) 'Service needs of families of children with severe physical disability' *Child Care, Health and Development* 18 259-282